THREE PLAYS

THREE PLAYS

CREDO
IN WALKS BUD
TALES OF A JEWISH AMERICAN PRINCE

GLENN LASZLO WEISS

Epigraph Books
Rhinebeck, New York

Paperback ISBN 978-1-960090-16-4

Library of Congress Control Number 2023909112

Book and cover design by Colin Rolfe

Epigraph Books
22 East Market Street, Suite 304
Rhinebeck, New York 12572
(845) 876-4861
epigraphps.com

CONTENTS

Norma Jean Howland in CREDO
Photo credit: Alex Smith

CREDO

A PLAY DICTATED BY MUSIC
GLENN LASZLO WEISS

CREDO

CREDO was first presented by the Vernon-Jackson Vision on March 6, 1989 at the University of the Streets on East 7th Street, New York City and was directed by the author with the following cast:

CHOCK Fullowitz . . . . John (Jay) Haran
TAG Omen . . . . .Ty Henderson
CHILERA Spite . . . . Norma Jean Howland
GOLDIE T . . . . Elizabeth Pressman
CONNIE Edwards . . . . Thomas Davison

Music was from contemporary adaptations of Thelonious Monk's music. Invaluable assistance was provided by Michel Stuart.

Author's Note: Written to pieces of music, especially scenes titled i.e. The Terrors, The Passions, etc. Collaborators should feel free to choose what music they want and where.

TIME AND PLACE:

A brief period of time following a crisis in the mind and life of CHOCK Fullowitz.

CHOCK is a thirtyish Jewish Man with a manic/depressive range of emotions, movements and thoughts. He has a fleeting nature.

CHILERA is a mid-twenties part American Indian woman who can be both spiteful and very giving within the same moment. She has a vulnerable nature.

TAG is a thirtyish black male who is wise and knowing. He represents a positive force in CHOCK's life. He has an artistic and romantic nature.

GOLDIE T. is a Jewish woman in her thirties. She is passionate and above all, pragmatic. She is extremely capable of getting everything done.

CONNIE is an insidious, puzzling and negative force. Only CHOCK is aware of his presence.

BEGINNING

(TAG is discovered on the telephone as lights come up.)

TAG

He jumped into a plate glass window? Problems, no. Grass, a little. No, not a problem. No. Oh, every day. Huh, five or six years, yeah. Jobs, hundreds of them, about a day or so. Shows, yeah, a few. What? Tell people. Who? Don't know that he had any friends. Chock, the Great Isolator. There's just the lady he lived with. OK. Be there. Bye. (Hangs up)

[BLACKOUT]

(TAG with CHILERA in a room.)

CHILERA

He started listening to that music, Working with it. Brought problems on. Stopped relating to people. Felt against the grain of the world. Drove five hundred miles in different directions to find another place to live. Came back. Lower each time. Ran out of places to run from himself.

TAG

Sounds like premonitions of disaster. If you got the music in your head. And the noise, the words you need a foundation to withstand it. When I go out there and play my ax, night after night, I buffer my soul from the pain. Naturally and unequivocally. I went through the fire again and again. Chock doesn't even remotely have the inner protection. With the noise in his head, it was a sheer premonition of disaster right from the start.

[BLACKOUT]

(CHILERA and CHOCK alternate lines, phrases as marked. CHILERA is where we left her. CHOCK is in a hospital bed with his head bandaged. CONNIE is by CHOCK enacting images of speech where appropriate.)

CHOCK	CHILERA
It's like a feeling that comes over you	
	A blanket of numbness.
When everything flows to the top. When you know that the last drop of concern	
	for life around you has vanished. Into thin air.
When you see the person you were.	Is now a zombie.
When everything comes to a head	A sleepwalker.
You call out to the person.	As if looking for vital signs.
You try to determine Whether there is any relationship to....	What once was awake.
Where you were at the point of embarking on a life.	What once was so alive that he carried me away.
A life where you had an idea. Big ideas.	Now has stuffed, stifled and en- sconced me.
That led to trouble.	To what I can only call an early grave. A Nightmare.
That led to sedation.	Which gives me an attitude

CHOCK

Misguided self-preservation.

Getting numb saved me for a while. The desire to hurl oneself at a window was always there.

The permeation to the soul
of a force driving you to
hide. Beseeching you to run.
Bemoaning the bridges you have
burnt.

Exit signs everywhere. The craving to get out of your skull. Away from the pounding thoughts.

Then a point where you cannot get out. Where the only thrill is finding the drug, not using it. IT DOESN'T WORK ANYMORE! Now always ragged. Always inadequate. Permanent dis-ease.

CHILERA

Of a very unforgiving nature.

Dark shadows. Instead of sunlight. Blinds already drawn.

Pretending everything's O.K. Believing it to be true. But knowing life is turning out all wrong.

Feeling that I'm going insane. That I can fix everything. A roaring insecurity that paralyzed my movement. Movement not away but toward the insanity.

A marking of two paths gone awry. Beyond a point of cohesion. Beyond rationality,

CHOCK	CHILERA
	excuse, justification. A repetition of family background. Father, a drunk. Mother, I don't know what? Shotguns going off in the dark house. Siblings scattered from the Arctic to the Equator. Feeling all this inside.
Months, years, you can't remember. Lots of scenes inflicted upon loved ones, colleagues, powers that be. The destruction of all that you embarked on. A perpetual scowl. A clenched face etched in bewilderment.	

[BOTH SIMULTANEOUSLY:]

CHOCK

Your mind says "Jump." You jump.

CHILERA

This is it! This is how it ends.

TOGETHER

Then you wake up in a strange room. With a whole new set of circumstances. Pieces of shattered glass is what's left of your life. You both try to begin all over again. Though you're very tired. You try again.

[FADEOUT]

(TAG and CHOCK in a hospital room.)

TAG

Wanna clue me in. What happened?

CHOCK

It was the night before. I made a decision. A decision to end my life.

TAG

Why?

CHOCK

It all seemed so pointless. Failure. I couldn't live with it anymore. No prospects as a director. No stability. Driving Chilera crazy.

TAG

Help? Why didn't you just ask for help?

CHOCK

I couldn't. That just isn't part of my makeup. I could say that I'm miserable but asking for help? I didn't know how. A man's supposed to . . . take care of things. As everything slipped away . . . I don't know. Everyone else was getting things done. Just couldn't even start. Just berated myself and Chilera started to get on me . . . over and over again. It's not her fault, though. I understand. I was just floundering . . . I . . . I'm so tired.

TAG

I'll let you sleep. I'll go talk to Chilera.

[BLACKOUT]

(CHILERA and TAG. She's packing.)

CHILERA

I'm getting out of here before Chock gets out of the hospital.

TAG

No, don't do that. He'll need you more than ever.

CHILERA

He'll need me more than ever? He always needs me more than ever.
He needed me when he went crazy. When he stopped participating in
life. When he stopped working and stopped trying to get a job. When
he just got high all the time. When he stopped buying food. When he
stopped paying the rent. When he stopped dealing with his family. His
family that never accepted me. When he stayed home all the time and
bombarded me with his problems, his crises, which were never ending.
When he demanded I listen in rapt attention to all his fantastic dreams
and plans that kept us up all night. That he was never even going to
begin because he was so mentally out to lunch. Now, he needs me more
than ever.

TAG

Don't go. Chock will come around. He is a survivor. Even a plate glass
window couldn't stop him. He loves you. He just got lost for a while. A
little understanding can go a long way.

CHILERA

I don't think I have any left. I need to take care of me, now. I got so
sidetracked with his problems. I want a career. I need to devote myself
to my acting, not to a maniac who suffocates me with his "I want, I
want" litanies.

(She goes to leave)

TAG:

But you love him, right? (Blocks her) (She nods, breaks down) Stay.
Wait.

CHILERA

Just for a little while.

[BLACKOUT]

(TAG, CHILERA and CHOCK [bandaged and in wheelchair]
enter from hospital. CHOCK runs from the others as TAG and
CHILERA blend in with CONNIE and GOLDIE who are the
voices, walkers and dancers in this scene. They create the impression
of multitudes of people going by involved with their situations.)

VOICE 1

So, we're going to have my cousins over.

VOICE 2

Why can't the ol' Prez just tell the truth. Since he's gonna die, he doesn't
want anyone to live past him.

VOICE 3

Capital gains are the most vital aspect to freedom for any individual.
Don't you agree?

VOICE 4

Actually, what I believe...

CHOCK

Put it on the shelf, they said. Put it all on the shelf.
    (Hugs self)

VOICE 5

I run drug centers. Treatment centers for drug addicts. And with what
the government is planning to do, throw money at the problem. Why, I
am in a position to make a fortune. You'll see. A fucking fortune!

    (All four actors converge in movement on each other and break
    apart. Stage is littered with confusion.)

CHOCK

Free at last! Free! Now how do I get from here to there? Do I even
want to?

TAG

Bread, soup, nuts, family.

CHILERA

Job, clock, rhythm, crises.

CHOCK

Put it on the shelf, they said. Just put it on the shelf.

TAG

Trains, motion, bullshit, fear.

CHILERA

Why did you do it? What did I do? How can you make me feel this way?

CHOCK

Put it on the shelf, they said. Put it on the.. .(angry) What? I was overwhelmed. Needed escape. You were there. You don't understand.

CHILERA

And what you did to me? I held you up for years and then you give me this?

(Tempo quicker. The following is repeated)

TAG	CHILERA
Money, bread, soup, dread.	What did you give me but problems? All I Did was pay and make excuses for you.
Hate, fear, no love there.	
FEAR, FEAR, FEAR, FEAR.	

CHOCK

Put it on the shelf, they said. Put all of it on the shelf. Put all...of it...on the...they...said...Put it...put it... on.

[BLACKOUT]

(CHOCK runs into TAG on the street.)

TAG

Whoa, slow down, man. You're really charged up.

CHOCK

I just got out of this place.
(Catches breath)
You know, the hospital sent me there. It's like medicine. We talk about what we're going through. All kinds of people with the same problems. It makes me want to live.

TAG

That's great. Just keep doing it, kid. I gotta run uptown. See you later.

CHOCK

Yeah, before you go. Wait.
(pause)
I just want to say, well... I need Faith and Patience. I mean, I've been lost for along time.

TAG

Hey, we all do. We gotta do the best we can. Just keep going there, Chock. You'll be able to do what you always wanted. A job and your work in the theater. Love, all that stuff. Gotta run.
(exits)

CHOCK

It would take a miracle, I think.

[BLACKOUT]

[THE MARCH OF TREPIDATION.]

(CHOCK and CONNIE Edwards wrestle. CHOCK alternately breaks free, runs and flounders as CONNIE reaches him and smothers him. This action continues through the scene over and over.

CHOCK

Here I go...
Time to face our problems each day
To be productive, responsible

(CHILERA appears, disappears)

CHOCK

Hold my end up
   (falls)

CONNIE

With what? You're a loser. Feel sorry for yourself. Come on. You're good at that. You don't add up. You live off others. Go hurt somebody!
   (Pounces)

CHOCK

Here I go
I got some attributes.
I want to give. To create. To love.
   (he falls).

CONNIE

With what? You got nothin'. You ain't shit! You got one thing in your mind. To run. To get the fuck out of here. Check out. Fuck everything and run. Ain't that the way it is? Now, you got it F.E.A.R.
   (Laughs 5 beats and exits).

CHOCK

Here I go...

CHOCK CONT.

I got nothing. I'm a raw nerve. The world can fling me around. But I gotta try. Here I go.

(He knocks on door, shaking)

[BLACKOUT]

(In middle of stage. CHOCK is surrounded by TAG and CHILERA, with CONNIE behind him elevated.)

CHOCK

I've cried a river of tears. No more. I refuse. If I'm bound to have euphoria and depression as my common themes, so be it. But they said, NO! NO! NO! How long, do I have to hear that? How can people go on with that ringing in their ears. NO! So definite.

TAG

I remember I was seven years old. My uncle brought me to this impresario to launch my career. He looked at me and said, "Don't bring me a boy, bring me a man." That was it. I cried. Later I read how Bud Powell played with the greats at eleven. Now I'm a man and it's not any easier. I see kids getting more chances.

CHILERA

You can't just check out, Chock. I mean, you could, but it takes a lot more courage to get through the pain and rejection and get to somebody saying "YES!" Not that it's happened to me, yet, but...

CHOCK

Platitudes. Bud got beaten on his head. His spirit broke. Chilera, how many yesses have you ever gotten?

TAG

No man, it's attitudes. You're not the first nor the last. Not the best nor the worst. Hear.

(All four characters branch out to their own spaces and separate pools of light. CONNIE sticks close to CHOCK. TAG and CHILERA are getting ready to go out. TAG is preparing to play at a club. CHILERA to go onstage. CONNIE is preparing to tempt CHOCK with drugs. Their movements should support their preparations.)

(Movements are wild, explosive, sensual. They are illustrative of the struggle, fight and rebellion necessary to throw off The Weight of Reality.)

TAG

I know this kid (meaning Chock). He gives everything he's got to whatever he does. He takes hardship heavy, though. He acts like he's born yesterday, you know what I mean? He don't know about life. He never accepted the moment when you decide; what you're doing, what you're about. He's there, though, as much as he can be, for his friends. Those he has. But the thing is he never picked up on those things, you know. Sanity, Stability and Responsibility.

CONNIE

He got a hole where you supposed to be full. He got himself a woman and he don't know why! Just took her hostage. Makes demands. "Do everything for me and I'll tell you things that justify your existence. Just make love and bring the money home. Shelter me from people who push my buttons. I'll just go to the park and cop my weed everyday and that'll be my true lover, friend and you'll just be there for me. Don't look to me for anything. But don't worry, I'll still be here and that's enough for you."

CHILERA

Now you're coming alive. I want to live with you. But you gave me all of your attitudes. OH-I HATE LIFE! Everything is doomed. Failure and helplessness is all there is to life. I don't feel anything and now you're beginning to feel. How unfair. When you were a zombie I had control. It always was your fault. I feel more comfortable taking care of someone and having all the responsibility. It's wrong. I know. But it's all I know. Now, I'm disgusted with your change. Alright, if it has to be - I need some Sanity, Stability and Responsibility from you - you fucker!

CHOCK

I want to be a great artist. With plenty of lovers, friends. Want a co-op in the city and a house in the country with a studio where I can bring all my collaborators upstate and work on all my projects. Money and art. I want. I burn for these things. Yeah and look at all the women, yeah. I'm awake now. And clothes, clothes all kinds - I need that plastic card, man. Life is heavy but I got a place to go to. It soothes me — gets me to see Sanity, Stability and Responsibility - so sweet!

(TAG and CHILERA are in shock at CHOCK's words. CONNIE laughs

(TAG goes to bus stop to play at club. He passes CHOCK en route. CHILERA rehearses lines to herself, moves past CHOCK and hails taxi in view of CHOCK. CONNIE ambles over to CHOCK. He looks CHOCK square in the eye and nods three times and exits laughing. CHOCK goes to drugs, drops them instead goes to phone and calls GOLDIE who is seen on upper stage left with phone.)

CHOCK

I can't do it. Sanity, stability and responsibility
        (repeats like a death sentence)
I'm so lonely.

GOLDIE

(Smiles as she says Magic Words)

I understand, baby.

[FADEOUT]

(CONNIE holding a fishbowl and continually rubbing it as he speaks. Puts bowl down and does conjuring dance at will. Then repeats.)

CONNIE

There are those that CRAVE, CRAVE, CRAVE. They'll do anything to satisfy it. But the joke is that's impossible. There are those that THRIVE, THRIVE, THRIVE. On those that CRAVE. Satisfaction Guaranteed. Ever hear of that? What a laugh. Those that CRAVE—CAN ONLY THINK OF THEMSELVES. That's the crux of it. DELUXE SELFHOOD.

Hello, I'm CONNIE Edwards. I UNDERSTAND your self-pity. I KNOW how to fill your void. I can make you feel like you don't stick out. I UNDERSTAND! OW! YEAH! Don't that turn you on? Whatever gets you through the night. Yeah. WHATEVER. Drugs, Drink, Food, Love, Sex, Etcetera. To FEED THE SELF. THE SELF.

WHEN YOU CRAVE to free yourself from SELF, SELF, SELF. I THRIVE, THRIVE, THRIVE, You tortured and wretched beings.

All you gotta do is close the door. Go to the window and see there is more to life than yourself, DIG? But I'll never tell.

THINK I'M STUPID OR SOMETHING!

[BLACKOUT]

(TAG and CHOCK are walking on the street.)

CHOCK

I don't know, man, it's like I used to go down the block to get high - now I sneak away to cry.

TAG

It's time for a look back and no copping out!

(Stage becomes a labyrinth made up of five actors with CHOCK in the middle. They are all extensions, attitudes and projections of his background. Actors go to their opening places during the following scene. GOLDIE unsheathes scroll. TAG sets table for hotel scene. CHILERA gets into burlesque costume. CHOCK goes down "block", turns indecisively, moves stage right, then stage left. He picks up attitude of moving ahead, then gives up. He starts to run off—stage but is halted by GOLDIE's opening lines.)

GOLDIE
(unrolling sheaf of papers)

CHOCK Fullowitz, an only child. Spoiled rotten and pampered all your life. Now deal with who you are!

GOLDIE AS MOTHER

You are just like your father. Can't do anything. A disappointment, a failure. No. Don't promise us anything because you won't show up.

CHOCK

It's a math and science school, ma. I hate that stuff. I want to be in the theater. I'm just going because you want me to.

MOTHER

So, isn't that how it should be? Besides, how can you be a doctor or lawyer if you fool around with the the-a-ter?

CHOCK
(to audience)

There was always screaming in the house. Not arguing. My parents would always say, "We're discussing, that's all." And they'd be screaming. Later on, the music would cover the screaming. Just tune me out.

MOTHER

Where are you going, Chock? At this hour.

CHOCK

Out, ma. I gotta get out.

(To audience)

I could never stay in. Always out. To what? don't know. I was always the first. First, to try drugs. First, to dare to do something outrageous.

(TAG and CHOCK)

CHOCK

Let's do something. I got it, let's sneak into the hotel.

TAG

What, are you crazy?

CHOCK

Yeah come on, we'll watch the comedian and when he bombs, you know those pickles, they got on the tables?

(Mimes throwing pickles)

Boom!

(In hotel)

CONNIE

(As Comic)

Even the mustard seeds held their noses.

(Pause)

(CHOCK throws pickles).

Hey—get that kid!

(TAG and CHOCK run out. TAG goes off.)

CHOCK
(To audience)
They took me to the sheriff's office. I laughed for hours, even though I was in all this trouble. It was frightening. Always the first. Until we started to grow up and had to make decisions. Big decisions. Like relationships.

(Topless Bar)

CHILERA
(sashaying)
Gonna get me a Jew, a doctor, an Injun chief. Hi baby, I'm one-half Cherokee, you know. Like my body. Like my shiksa face?

CHOCK
Never saw anyone like you. I need a doctor. Think I'll self-prescribe.

CHILERA
This is my whole story, baby. I've been abandoned. On my own since I'm fourteen. I don't dig the straight and narrow. Trouble is my middle name. I'll make you dance in bed. No mamma's boys for me. Wanna try?

MOTHER
Remember Abigail, Chock, you played with her when you were five years old. She's taking business courses. She can help you. You need someone to help you face life.

CHOCK
(Engrossed with Chilera, addresses audience)
Me? I don't need anyone. I know where I'm going.

CHOCK
(Staring at Chilera)
Never seen anyone like you. Yeah. I'm pretty wild, too.

(Home)

CHOCK

Ma, this is my friend, Tag. He's a musician.

MOTHER

A Schwartze? And a musician? What kind of...

CHOCK

I'm going to California.
(To audience)
Always running. And taking myself with me. Working my ass off. Filled with dissatisfaction. Fights with my peers and the press.

(California)

CHOCK

I submit to all of you, the press. I have done sixteen productions in one year. Covered every aspect of theatrical presentation. Given my whole being to my art and there has been a CONSPIRACY AMONG YOU ALL TO PUT ME IN UTTER OBLIVION!

CONNIE

(The Press)
We do not recognize anyone who has not resided in our fair city for at least five years.

CHOCK

(Sitting, directly to audience)
So, I responded. With Fuck You. Very adult, very accepting. See, I had it all. Complete artistic control, money to do what I wanted and friends, good friends. But I had nothing underneath...no substance. So I said, Fuck you and got high.

CHOCK CONT.

(To Chilera)

All my life I've been misunderstood. You understand me, baby. Don't you?

CHILERA

You influenced me like no other. You've taught me about life, art, people, everything. But you have a poison in you. You want to destroy yourself.

CHOCK

I'm going home for a few days.

(To audience)

And the past slapped me hard in the...I had a great romance in the past. Another ideal was shattered.

GOLDIE

(As Becky)

You remember, honey, when I was fifteen and you were nineteen. You wouldn't put it in me. I've been thinking, dreaming about it all these years, and I have only one thought. I WANT TO FUCK YOU! Let's get high and do it!

CHOCK

(Holding onto wall)

DON'T RUIN THE PICTURE! NO!

(He gives in. They embrace. Next day.)

CHOCK

(Back against wall)

I promise to step on everyone in my path from this moment on. I'm gonna run through this city.

(Kisses different women)

I will loathe everyone, myself included, until I've turned myself into nothing.

(Hangs up phone, slams door, lies down and hits self).

CHOCK CONT.

Now I deal.

(California)

CHILERA

I missed you so, honey.

CHOCK

Yeah, me too. I can't stay here. Everything is collapsing. The floor is giving way. I'm gonna run. Maybe to Canada, maybe Texas. I'm not comfortable here. I'm into a personality conflict with an entire city.

CHILERA

What about me? I'm doing important things for myself here. You expect me to follow you?

CHOCK

(To himself)
You can't follow me, where I'm going.
(To her)
No, baby, you stay here. I'll be all right.

CHILERA

I'll come when I finish. We love too much to be apart.

CHOCK

(To self)
No, it's between me and myself.
(To her)
No, I need you. Come!

CHILERA

Soon, honey, when I finish.

CHOCK

Could be too late.

[PAUSE]

CHILERA

I'm here, baby. Kiss me.

CHOCK

(In GOLDIE's arms)
I'm through, ma, I'm through! I don't know where I fit in.

CHILERA

I'm gonna leave you. It's been years and you can't get started. I'm holding you up. I can't stand it anymore. I have a life I want to make for myself. Dreams, hopes, aspirations and you are killing them all. Crawl into a hole and die, if you're so bent on destruction, but I can't go on like this.

(CHOCK and TAG)

TAG

Man, I can't relate to you. You don't want to live. You're not there for yourself.

(CHOCK shrugs)

GOLDIE

What a wasted life! What you could have been. I'm going where the money is. A dentist in Glen Cove. Excuse me, my life is waiting.

(CHOCK turns only half of his body as if to say, wait)

(CONNIE and CHOCK on a bench)

CONNIE

Now you got it. No more pain, no more remorse, just do it! No more victim bullshit. Not made for this world? Try the next one. Isolation, who needs it? You're a monster, anyway. Just close your eyes and run. Run straight through it, when it shatters, you will be FREE! Dig!

CHOCK

(Poised)

No one

(long pause)

understood.

[FADEOUT]

(CHOCK alone. Does not wear bandage for the first time)

CHOCK

I take responsibility

for choosing to be miserable

for having no faith

for running from life's terms

for causing pain to others

for hurting myself

for letting obsessions rule me. For refusing to grow up....

CHILERA

enters

Do the laundry, honey. Fifty-fifty, between us, now.

TAG

enters

My old man is dying, buddy. You gotta help me.

CONNIE

enters

Same old shit, man. Let's split this scene for good. You don't want sober references, now do you?

(He leads, CHOCK follows)

GOLDIE

enters

Come to me, baby.

(CHOCK pauses — FADEOUT)

END OF ACT I

ACT II — ORDER

THE PASSIONS
THE TERRORS
THE HATCHING
COFFEE SHOP
THE SHARE PART I
WHY CAN'T I FLY?
THE VENEER OF FEAR
CHOCK'S LAMENT
CHILERA'S POINT
THE BALANCE
PARTING DANCE
THE SHARE PART II
CHILERA - NEW MONOLOGUE
THE CALLING

ACT II

THE PASSIONS

CHOCK

(Intro)

My mind's going over the edge. Like over a cliff. Sometimes I awake with a start. Eyes bulging, all of me ignited. Down to the smallest nerve. Too alive for this body. Too alive for this world. I just want to burst out. Live, experience to the fullest. Drive my desires into abundant expression, you know? Know what I'm saying?

TAG

Feelings at full throttle. Lurching forward without direction. All consuming. I know. You've got to channel it. Mind going

CHOCK

Like over a cliff. Down the dark recesses. Passionate pessimism. Bleak, dismal dirges of this planet. Of the collective spirit. Cook into Desperation. And back out to the Wonder of Living. Magnificent Creation. Then... .stuck.

TAG

Stuck? Keep spinning it. It'll move.

CONNIE

(Hysterical)

This too shall pass? All is as it should be? It's meant to be. Be patient, it will get better. C'mon, what shit!

CHOCK

Out among Fields of Romance. Beautiful, moonlit initial contact with someone special. Friendship. Feelings glowing in togetherness mirroring a communal campfire. Huddled Warmth. Feeling safe, protected.

TAG

Sharing the pain. The Joy. Everyone playing their ax, communicating their insides in Harmonious Understanding.

CONNIE

(All broken up)
Relaaating. Iiiidentifying. Give me a break.

CHOCK

Coming back to early morning foggy confusion. My guts exposed like frayed wire. Scarred from living another day on strictly life's terms. A gamut of emotion spent.
(Passes out)

TAG

That's all we have. What we're given. Another day in the bank. Asking for help, if necessary. From people and a Higher Spirit. Solace. Peace. Serenity.
(Keeps going over prone CHOCK, fans him).

CONNIE

Crap!

TAG

You got it. You're on the right track. Just keep letting your noise out. Tomorrow.

[BLACKOUT]

THE TERRORS

(CHILERA and CHOCK. There is a cauldron of fire in the middle
of the stage. Open wings, left and right. Movement toward cauldron
and away to wings. Back and forth, respectively.)

BOTH

What do we do? We've been together so long? What do we feel?
We know each other so well. And not at all. Not one iota.
Do we start a new life? How? Where do we begin?

CHOCK

Everyone I meet turns me on. I come home. You treat me like the old
sonofabitch I used to be.

CHILERA

You are more of a sonofabitch than ever. Dry, misery-laden, unmitigat-
ed Hate. Towards me. More than ever.

BOTH

There's the open door.
No!
How?
Can't!
So ill-equipped.

[BLACKOUT]

THE HATCHING

(GOLDIE, CHOCK and TAG. Movement is child play. Scene takes place in theater workshop GOLDIE and CHOCK belong to. Others are onstage as audience. Scene should be improvisatory in feel or done as improv.)

CHOCK

We go to relationship counseling. Know what it means? More chores around the house.

GOLDIE

You gotta get away, baby. You're like a tea kettle about to boil. Let's hear you whistle.

CHOCK

Just like a Bogie movie.

GOLDIE

I'm your ear, kid. You can tell me all of it.

CHOCK

Well, it's like this...

GOLDIE

Not so close, huh. Remember sex for the first time? Pretend that I'm her, I'm all of them. We're hangin' out at the playground. Acting cool. Drinkin' and takin' those little red pills. What happens?

CHOCK

I always get in fights with men, not other kids, grown men.

GOLDIE

Where does it lead you?

CHOCK

A two year relationship. Like fighting with myself. No one can tell me anything. But through her, I found the theater. Missed my graduation. Was playing Chinese twins in a summer stock upstate. You know, Ching looking for Ling. Exit. Ling looking for Ching.

GOLDIE

A make believe world. Transported. Being other people. Heroes, romantic leads. Life is one big snow-covered, cherry-topped marquee of a mountain....Then...

CHOCK

My heart sank. Adulthood. Like a cat caught stuck up in a tree looking for the right place to land. Paralyzed.

TAG

You're messin' up. Someone's got to tell you. This is leadin' nowhere.

CHOCK

Integrity enters the picture. Uncompromising ideals. Ruins all the fun. Upholding images, Lenny Bruce, Dylan, Shepard.

GOLDIE

Joan of Arc, Patti Smith, Joan Rivers.

ALL 3

Joan Rivers?

GOLDIE

Well, I thought I was relating.

TAG

What it really is about today is...

ALL 3

Look at us today. Look how we walk. Look how we burn. Look how we duck. Look how we talk. Talk it out. Face it down. Spin it 'round. Grind it up. Like Steam. It Out. It Out. It Out.

[BLACKOUT]

COFFEE SHOP

(CHOCK and GOLDIE enter a "coffee shop"; a table on stage. They are laughing.)

GOLDIE

You didn't? No, you did?
(laughs)

CHOCK

Yeah,
(Laughs)
I really did. They said, "CHOCK, you're the leader. So, where do we go?" I said, "I'm the leader, right?" They said, "Yeah, right." I said, "You sure?" They said, "Yes." I said, "Alright, everybody, this way to Bellevue."
(They laugh)
Then two cops rode by on horses. And I swear, we thought it was the cavalry. Like there were two thousand cops, all looking for us in Central Park.
(They laugh)

GOLDIE

Not the good Jewish boy.

CHOCK

Never.

GOLDIE

I tell you, I feel . . . I don't know. Like we've gone through things together. Or we grew up together. Something . . . I don't know. When we're sitting in the workshop and we're both getting restless, you know, like we've gone past where the others are going and we look at each other and laugh. And then we're in collusion. . . subversive, but it's not that.

CHOCK

Well, maybe, we've both been around the block a couple of times.

GOLDIE

The thing is, I take everything so seriously. I mean all the time. Everything I do. I've given up a lot to come here and struggle to be an artist. And I don't cut up, crack up. That's not my style. But you get me going and suddenly you're more serious than me. "This is just masturbation," you say to the director. "That's utter self-indulgence". Then you drive us harder. Then I drive us harder. And yet, when we're sitting with the others we know that we're wasting our time.

CHOCK

It's just pure arrogance on my part and defeats what I'm trying to do there.

GOLDIE

Which is?

CHOCK

Participating in something without running the show. Taking criticism constructively. Contributing positively within a group.

GOLDIE

Is that what you are there for?

CHOCK

Yes. Do you understand?

GOLDIE

I do, but you are still who you are. And I like and appreciate you for that.

CHOCK

Thanks. The feeling is mutual.

GOLDIE

Look, I know how to behave. How to play the game. It's all bullshit, anyway. I can wear many hats to get what I want. I'm not that proud. I mean, I have principles, strong ones, but I'm not adverse to giving them what they want to get the part or to put the show on. I've learned how. Maybe while you were out there giving yourself a bad time I honed these skills. But you gotta learn to create your art, you can't let pride and principles get mixed up. It's simple. We may be similar inside but my outsides are more polished.

CHOCK

The innocence must die.

GOLDIE

Then let it die. Listen I belong to a group that is on a higher level than these people. I'd like to bring you there. You could make some connections, possibly.

CHOCK

That would be great. No one's ever done that for me.

GOLDIE

Oh, poor baby.
      (They laugh)
You really are full of yourself, Fullowitz.

CHOCK

And so are you, dear lady.

[BLACKOUT]

THE SHARE — PART I

(CHOCK alone.)

CHOCK

All night coffee shops. Talking and laughing. Hanging on to each others' words. Communicating like two souls who belong together. But am I just making a big deal out of something that regularly happens in life? There's certainly plenty of obstacles. There is something I would so much like to tell you, dear lady.

(TAG enters)

(To TAG:)

I sit in parks and listen to love songs. Think of GOLDIE. Endlessly. That's all I can do, seemingly do. When we work together, I am so inspired. But if I try anything - she's married - I'm like married. It's a smash-up. My only recourse is to talk about it. It's better than acting on my feelings in this situation. She's giving me new contacts. My work is progressing. It's who you know. That's what she always says. And she knows.

TAG

The benefits of becoming friends outweigh the trouble you'd cause if you made a move. You can always tell me about it. I'm here. That's what friendship is for. No matter how long it takes. I'm going to tell you something out of my life. There was this singer who came to town...

[BLACKOUT]

WHY CAN'T I FLY?

(Coffee Shop: CHOCK and GOLDIE.)

CHOCK

You're the only woman who gets me, who knows what I'm about, you know? I want to change things, the world, my art...

GOLDIE

Hold it.
(laughing)
What about yourself first?

CHOCK

Oh, but I am. Come here, GOLDIE, come closer.

GOLDIE

I can't. You know I'm married.

CHOCK

Yeah...look let's just collaborate on this project. Now the action turns on this...
(trails off)

(Later. CHOCK and GOLDIE out of an embrace. CHOCK jumps on a platform.)

CHOCK

You know, you move me baby. You make me fly. I get so full when I'm with you - so full - and then I die, just die.

GOLDIE

I met you too late. But that's the way it is. I'd like to fly, too but can't be - with you. Let's stick to the work. I'm such a jerk. But I am a realist.

CHOCK

We got to be fearless.
(grabs her)

GOLDIE

No!
(Pushes him away)
You'll see. You have to grow, get aware then you won't dare!

(He chases her around platform They run into CHILERA and TAG. TAG lifts CHILERA and in dance they make GOLDIE dance away.)

TAG

Stick to the home front, man. Don't turn dreams into reality when you can't back them up or you'll knock your head against a brick wall.
(CHILERA leaps over TAG into center.)
Your woman needs you man. Work at your relationship. You're starting all over. She's been with you, paid her dues, understand.

CHILERA

My soul beats for you. But I can't seem to do anything right by you. You won't sleep with me. Relate to me. Love me. Be sweet, is that too much to ask?

CHOCK

But I can't get any inspiration from it.

CHILERA

From us, you mean.

CHOCK

Yeah. Too many miles down the same road.

CHILERA

But now the road is clear.

CHOCK

I need a new one.

CHILERA

I'm yours. I've always been.

CHOCK

But I'm new and you're old...to me. I need new inspiration.

TAG

You mean a new distraction. That's what you mean. Go home, man. Ask yourself, is this worth giving up?

CHOCK

I can't, man.
  (To CHILERA)
Sorry.

  (TAG and CHILERA exit. CHOCK to corner and GOLDIE.)

CHOCK

Save my life.

GOLDIE

Only you can do that, baby. Besides, I've got my own.

CHOCK

We'll still work together.

GOLDIE

Count on it.

(Kisses him on cheek, exits).

[FADEOUT]

THE VENEER OF FEAR

(CHOCK alone. CONNIE enters.)

CHOCK

I'm broken, battered but not beaten.

CONNIE

Now you done it. You got nobody.

CHOCK

Get lost!

CONNIE

Another layer comes off, oh yeah.
Where's the veneer? That was here.
That warded off. All the warts.
That choked off the hurdles
And sequestered the fear.
What a crime. A heinous crime.
To rob oneself of the source of Pleasure.
By the Force of one's Nature.
Why the gloom? Why the doom?
No experience to share on the subject of Dare.
No risks taken.
Another layer shaken off.

TAG

Life! Can you feel it, my man? Makes you soar. Don't take it so serious.
Don't make it a chore!

CHOCK

Fall off the mountain. And land again and again.

CONNIE

Another layer off. Another crash landing. To feel the real Soul of the Human Core. Watch out! They come at you from all different directions.

[BLACKOUT]

CHOCK'S LAMENT

CHOCK

My story. Or the lack of it. Cry. Whisper. Let out the
guilt. See, my lady crumble. While I'm out there. Floundering
within a heartbeat. That knows not where it is going.
Feeling cursed. Feeling like a bad person.
All knotted up. Sliding down into a pit.
There I've been feeling. Not really knowing.
All screwed up and screwing everything up.
If I staged a scene
Between my woman and me.
There'd be a lot of disharmony.
If I stage a scene
From what she sees
It could not be. I can't see it.
Therein lies the problem. But I gotta try. Here goes.

(CHILERA comes on and does CHILERA's Point)

CHILERA'S POINT

CHILERA

I don't have a clue. Where I'm running. I just know I got to. Can't be there. Not for Jim, Slim or any other Him. I need to fly somewhere. Anywhere. Just don't need anyone hanging onto me. I got my own dreams. I see myself as someone in the middle of things. Someone necessary to make things work. With a purpose. A mission. Not beholding to anyone. A Higher Purpose. Not stupid, phony parties. Or business schemes. Or family bullshit. A Great Big Necessary Vital Essential SOMETHING that the world needs or it will just stop dead in its tracks. I need to break free of strangleholds on my soul by any individual, SEE!

(CHOCK backs away from CHILERA into TAG's Music Room. CONNIE hangs back, attempts to contribute but remains in role of eavesdropper as scene unfolds)

TAG

What's up? What's got you, man?
Seen a ghost? Wet your pants? Lost your best friend?
Sittin' here. Trying. Got a gig tonight.
They're buying, huh? Help me. Gotta get it right.

CHOCK

How can I help? Mood's crashing. No good to
Letting down CHILERA. Again. Powerless over
My passion's fucking up my work.

TAG

Shit. Have a laugh on me. Repeat after me. Relentless.
This is my song for tonight.

Life is so relentless.
Life is so strong, intractable.
Rolls right over your rage.

TAG

Punch the air and go on.
Let those phantoms out.
Reach whatever you can.

CHOCK

Relentless.
Relentless.
Relentless.
Relentless.
Relentless.

(CONNIE reacts badly)

CHOCK

Flip your horn and bond with the sky.

(CONNIE chokes)

TAG

Embrace your feelings
and rejoice in them.
Pull a chair out from under
your designs.

(CONNIE collapses)

CHOCK

Can't predict a result, if you try.
It's someone else's domain.
Or it can only be uphill.

49

Man, some heavy-duty rough terrain.

TOGETHER

Let's be wild within ourselves.
Keep daring to go higher.
Try to create from our souls
and always tell the truth
We've got this rage, this joy, this bond,
This Insanity.

(CONNIE slithers away)

[3]

If we don't laugh at ourselves.

CHOCK

I'm blocked.

(CONNIE sniffles)

TAG

I'm jammed.

CHOCK

I'll get to the bottom of it. All of it. And go on.

TAG

Chao, Maestro. Chao.

[BLACKOUT]

THE SHARE — PART II

TAG

I'm going to tell you something out of my life. There was this singer who came to town. We looked at each other and it was all over. Gone. Both of us. We had our separate situations. I would have died for one night with her. I created a lot of scenarios in my head about how it would happen. When it happened I wound up with my suitcase begging people to take me in, night by night. She went back to her old man's mansion in Grosse Pointe, Michigan. I could have spent the rest of my life with her. No problem. I could have died for her. No problem. She had a problem, though. She liked things the way they were. She would have done almost anything for me. We were very simpatico. Very attracted. She offered many positive prospects as long as I didn't act on what I felt. I couldn't stop myself. I was consumed with the thought of our lives together. Her life was already mapped out. What I was thinking and what she was thinking differed. My extent of thinking was obsession. Hers was, "What a lovely afternoon, it could be." I walked around with my horn and suitcase through frost, snow, sleet and rain for six months. At some point it finally reached me deep down inside that it wasn't worth it.

[PAUSE]

CHOCK

Talk to you tomorrow.

TAG

Yeah.

[BLACKOUT]

(CHOCK and CHILERA laying together. CHOCK is sleeping. Lights dim.)

CHILERA

Now that everything is dark and quiet. Now, maybe, I can finally express myself. To myself. I like the dark. Nothing is exposed. I'm not threatened by the dark, Chock. I need to say a few things, just a few. About a little girl in a green nightdress in the night on a farm in the West with her hands over her ears because of the noise from her house crashing into the stillness and silence of the open land outside. You're not the only one with feelings, Chock. And about the woman who wants so much to be living her dream of who she wants to be and how nothing comes easy and you're pulled in one direction and then get reversed by the distraction of mere survival. Disappointment, frustration, deep swallow, hold breath. Having freedom of choice and yet none at all. Fed up, yet just getting ready to begin. Skipping, turning, twisting in one spot and poised to move to another. Waiting, wailing. Getting to the dream or lurching back to the same nowhere quicksand. Chock, you run into walls with such fury while I twist and cringe in my own river and SCREAM (he wakes up, watches) and deep down, real deep down, still see, still feel...the girl on the farm in the green nightdress, whipping in the wind in the dark. Swallowed up by others. And dreaming of only HERSELF.

(They touch and hold in a friendly manner.)

(Fadeout)

THE CALLING

(TAG comes on stage and speaks. A Dancer, who is CHOCK's Muse and could be danced by actress playing GOLDIE, if capable, moves to speech. CHOCK may or may not be on stage watching as piece goes on. It is not a good idea to have him participate in movement. At any rate, CHOCK, CHILERA and GOLDIE join in with TAG on last line of speech and play.

TAG

Sometimes. We have a calling: something we must do. Doesn't matter, the cost, the pain, the humiliation... I've been there since I was four. People don't understand. They go on in their set ways, they don't see, only what's in front of them. They have no peripheral vision. They don't FEEL the scene, the entire scene, man. It can put you out in the cold. Where no one really wants to be. Where it's not safe. Where you get no approval. No one goes out of their way. No one seeks you out. But... If my man can accept it. That his choices add up to being on the edge. That there is no sentimentality involved. No self—pity. It is just the way it is. And still function in this world. Then we will hear from him. He'll go somewhere.

And find like souls. It just takes time.., and his work might touch those with their heads down...moving straight ahead. Reproducing their lives...keeping up with the status quo. Following a line...down the line. Making sure they don't speak too loud...maybe, my man will get them to look away.. .for a moment.

(Repeated three times)

Sometimes...

We have a calling.

If we don't destroy ourselves...

And live...and live...and remain in one piece.

[CURTAIN]

From L to R: Arthur French, Arlana Blue and John-Martin Green in IN WALKS BUD.
Photo credit: Jon Slaff

IN
WALKS
BUD

GLENN LASZLO WEISS

IN WALKS BUD

IN WALKS BUD was first presented by Inner Fires Co. in conjunction with LaMaMa, ETC. Ellen Stewart, Producer on February 2, 1996 at LaMaMa 74A East 4th Street, New York City and was directed by the author with the following cast:

Thelonious Monk . . . . Arthur French
Bud Powell . . . . John-Martin Green
Nica . . . . Arlana Blue

Music was composed by Kenny Barron and Geri Allen. Music was played for the production by Geri Allen and later Richard Thompson.
Set by Inigo Elizalde
Lights by Yun Young Koo
Sound by Tim Schellenbaum
Production Stage manager was Shelli Aderman
Invaluable Assistance was provided by Jack Zeman.

TIME:

New Year's Eve, 1964 (December 31, 1963). It is hours preceding a Thelonious Monk concert at Lincoln Center and hours following the concert.

PLACE:

Nica's, the jazz baroness' house in Weehawken, New Jersey. The play takes place in the living room. The room is represented by a couch center stage a piano is in the stage left corner and the rest of the room is covered by a glass effect, the back having the New York City skyline. Sound should suggest the wind blowing and glass shattering when the action calls for it later. NICA speaks from a stool stage right. The scene between MONK and BUD following her speech should be in shadows as in a dream that MONK is slowly stirring from. When the action starts in "real time" after the dream sequence, BUD has arrived from MONK's dream, summoned from MONK's deepest recesses.

CHARACTERS:

THELONIOUS MONK: age 46, a gentle bear of a man, not prone to discussing his inner workings but when exposed, utterly determined to search for answers. Riding the cusp of fame after many years of isolated rejection. A man searching for peace.

BUD POWELL: age 39, a combustible force given to thorough lethargy. A man, on his last legs and knows it. Though he has trouble staying focused, his purpose gives him uncharacteristic stamina. A child in a man's body, he yearns with all his being to make good for once on a human level.

BARONESS PANNONICA de KOENIGSWARTER (NICA): age 50, a real baroness, she is commonly known as the jazz baroness. Well—known for the scandal created when Charlie Parker died in her hotel room. A great friend to the jazz musicians who are her pride and passion. She is fiercely independent, very well educated and has felt ostracized her whole life for her oddities which boil down to a life dedicated to nonconformity and an overly intellectual approach to speech and thought. She has a British, Austrian and Hungarian background and is totally devoted to Monk. Their relationship is platonic.

NICA

Maybe it happened, maybe not. Some will swear it couldn't. They will produce affidavits that Bud Powell was in a sanatorium for tuberculosis in Paris at the time of the concert. It will say so in black and white. And who can argue with anything stated in black and white? There will be those who will argue that Bud could not walk at the time, not talk and was incapable of finding his nose let alone his only friend in seclusion during a New Year's snowstorm. There will be those who will insist Thelonious was securely home, in his home, not mine and basking in the glow of success that had finally arrived despite his disdain for all the trappings that come with it. They will undoubtedly say, how could he go into the darkness of seclusion upon finally realizing this hardly known bliss? A composer-pianist about to play before thousands with a full—blown orchestra to help usher in the New Year triumphantly swinging. They will say how improbable, how preposterous it would seem that a disheveled, sickly, downtrodden man of yesteryear be summoned to intrude upon this harmonious scene? Except that I know what I know. Thelonious was hiding out. He was away from his family that he loved dearly. And it was by choice. He was immensely troubled this night by demons which he could barely see and could only feel the slight impressions of their footfalls. He was remotely aware of an eerie disquiet. Uniquely, telepathically, he delivered the only one he could reach out to. The one who could identify the source of this particular madness. A howl, a cry in the night enjoined the men. The tranquility shattered, they faced each other. I was there. I dispute the so-called facts. They were together. There was the interruption of the work, of time and of space. Then life resumed. Changed. It was an all-nighter. It took a long time. It felt like a long time. The air was charged. Spirits were besotted in laughter and sadness. Wills, egos collided, they crashed forever insanity-tinged. Until the wind swept it all away. The tussle of Will was broken in two. It was morning. The ghastly splinters of shared pain were swept back into their proper places until another time, another place. A calming rain began and flooded out the residue caught hold in the snow. On the banks of New Jersey, I was there, my cats were there. We witnessed the session blowing hot, hotter than any of the arrangements played across the Hudson earlier that night at Lincoln Center. The men scoffed at the world's heralding of a New Year, when the real beginnings of their personal endings were taking shape. The public was lagging behind the artist again, they mused. I was there, I tell you. Their last meeting. Bud had to make it. He couldn't disappoint. He had some dues to pay. Thelonious had called him, though he didn't really know it himself. That is, until the damn thing had happened. Open your minds, dear friends and experience pain giving birth to solace. And something more? We will see, I assure you.

BLACKOUT

THELONIOUS MONK (laying on a couch)

MONK

Restless sleep, years fly by, they go back, always go back. I see chords written on so many walls. Bud's chords. Shadows filled with eyes, witnesses to the brutality. The years like weights pressing down on my buddy. The restless sleep full of years spinning 'round and finally stops at 1945.

(BUD POWELL in the shadows moving towards the lights.)

BUD

Floating across the water. Across time. Gasping, more like grasping to get a hold of ... mind sees Monk everywhere in my mind, I see him all the time. Feel him all the time. Going back to the scene of the first time all the trouble starts. Feel the crash, the crunch. Knuckles crashing on my head, so many of them. Mind back, mind bent backwards to the beginning of it all.

MONK

See, I stood up for this cat Bud. He came into the club where I was
house pianist, Minton's up in Harlem. He had some strange ideas on
that piano and of course, so did I. Knew what it was 'bout when someone was treated strange. So, I looked out for him, stood up for him
when people wanted him off the stand. Guess Bud got the idea he had
to do the same damn thing for me.

BUD

See, I'd seen and heard them say things behind my man's back. And it
burned me up. I caught them, yeah. Whispering, sneering and making sounds with their mouths and noses. Laughing, always laughing.
Sounded like the devil's chorus and I jumped, man, I jumped into the
fire! Lost where I was at. Thought I was in a club with Monk but I was
somewhere else. Just me and the cops and a bunch of steam and loud
whistles. Couldn't keep my mouth shut. I was so headstrong, mind was
strong back then and I walked like a god. Proud, so proud. Couldn't stay
back (lights up, BUD thinks he's in a club in Philadelphia, 1945. He
sees hecklers bothering MONK and intercedes) Hey, who you think
you're speaking to. This man is the father of us all. Don't dig his sound,
split. But if you dig me or somebody else you're paying heavy to see—
we learned at his side. (whips himself up) That's right, stay back before I
smoke you all out. I usually do it on the keys but this time I'll just ham-
mer you all out. (Stares) How 'bout the old face-down. Wait, shit how
many of you are there? Monk, I don't know, maybe I stepped into it
too deep (cowers, blows are raining on him) now, I ain't a fighter, just a
player, best goddamn one around. Oh, shit, even more are coming, hey,
you're supposed to be the police, supposed to protect me, not kill me!
Stop! Please, stop! Just a musician, man, God! No! (lights out on BUD).

MONK

Trouble was, Bud was in a lonely old train station, not a club. And no
one was 'round who knew him. I was only there in his mind.

BUD

How 'bout an acid bath? the man says. YEOW!!!

MONK

And there it all started. Could trace all of my buddy's problems from right there. Later, more beatings,

(BUD moans)

baths in ammonia,

(BUD screams)

driving out the spirit, the greatness, killing that man who danced into a room and made us all drop in awe of those hands. So fast and dancing. Lightning hands. I'd like to dance for you, man. All I can do today. Life goes on and we do the best.

(BUD makes a haunting sound)

Never the same. Fighting mediocrity. Everything against you, man from that time on. You were just a boy but the dues were paid as a man.

(BUD whimpers)

Playing it all out for the rest of our time.

(BUD roams stage freely moving in his own insanity, his voice should turn into reverberation last five or so lines which wake Monk from his sleep on couch and take us into present.)

BUD

Once upon a time in the furthest reaches of the mind. In everywhere land or more like Philly in 1945. Brakes on, what a pity! Ridicule was the game those goons played, those who didn't understand and laughed, laughed, laughed! Got no patience for this game . . . no patience, brakes on-don't follow through. But I must, an artist must! Stand up for my friend, all artists, we must stand for our friends, all true friends. This friend doesn't need any intervention. Just wants me to carry on with the invention, I have, all I have only that . . . save my courage, body, mind, yes, there's a lifetime to recover from this incident. No!

(Lights fade out and come back up as MONK awakes on couch in NICA'S living room).

(Scene: MONK laying out on couch. A tapping is heard. The wind blows the door open. There is the sound of leaves followed by music then the tapping resumes while MONK speaks and looks about).

MONK

What's that? Where's it coming from? Sounds like a note. A note to where? From where? The dreams, must be one. Nightmares? No, it's real. Happening. Only one can play those notes. Quit playing, Bud. Bud? Bud! Bud, is that really you? Don't see any notes on the walls. No, none on the water. But it's him. The one I know best. And it's been so long since I've seen him. Bud, is this really you? Got me going here and there. Why, 'cause he's Bud. Numero uno, man. Even though I'm the one playing tonight, in 'bout two hours. Where the hell are you? Trying to steal my thunder? As usual. He used to be lightning fast now only bottled lightning he's got goes by the name Thunderbird. Been listening, man. Sheeit. You can't hide it, even way overseas. I can hear you!

(BUD POWELL crashes through the door, cool but disheveled, with a bad cough and erratic energy).

BUD

Hey, Monk, get away from them curtains, get your ass away from that window. Shit, don't you know I've got some tippity-toes on my tail. Shit!

MONK

Bud! Hey! What the blazes this about?

BUD

Ran out on some doctors. Skipped.

MONK

Skipped?

BUD

Yeah. In Paris. Took me a long walk, all the way to New Jersey. Shit. Across the water. Hey! But seems like the secret's out. Got us some company.

MONK

What do you owe, Bud?

BUD

Same old Monk! Knows me like a book. Alimony, doctor bills, shit, you name it.

MONK

I name it right about where we left off.

BUD

Hey!

MONK

Hey! 1951. The Tombs. That ring a bell?

BUD

What do you think? Am I your brother in arms. Sheeit!

(They hug).

MONK

Well, it's safer now. Here. That's for damn sure.

BUD

Hey, not so, not necessarily so. I'm more comfortable over there.

MONK

Well, I've been in the lap of luxury over here.

BUD

Don't I know it.

MONK

Don't run me down now, pal. You know I paid the dues.

BUD

Man, you've paid them longer than anyone I've known. Hope it hasn't taken its toll like I've been hearing about, Monk.

MONK

What you mean? I'm just 'bout fit as a fiddle. Someone's been jivin' you, man.

BUD

Heard you aint been right, my friend.

MONK

Now I told you that's a bunch of jive. Give it up, drop it, man. I'm playing at Lincoln Center in a couple of hours with a full-blown orchestra, the tops, man. Does that sound like somebody out of their skull, Jack? Ten motherfucking piece band, man, you dig?

BUD

Hey, can't complain about that.

MONK

Hey!

BUD

Hey, now, that's it. Wait a minute. Where's Nica? I have an idea. (NICA enters, bringing a box of hats of all sizes, shapes and kinds). Hey, Nica, darling. Will you see to this tippity-toes outside?

NICA

Sure, Bud. What do you want me to do? Monk, doll, the hats from all over the world have arrived, which do you prefer today? This is a daily occurrence, Bud. Two deliveries. One is the order we put in, the other the ones the fans have sent to the office. Isn't it a trip?

BUD

(BUD grabs a few, nervously trying them on by mirror.)
Sure is, Lady N, here's what you tell them. Say, get off, this here's diplomatic property. Like you don't have any right to be on it. Like it's espionage. Like you're contraband in this here situation and you've got no protection. Use that European high-brow jazz, darling, hey! And baby, may I say it's a pleasure to see you.

NICA

Righto. I'll take care of it, Bud and then we'll catch up on the pleasantries.

BUD

Gotcha! Oh, and Lady N . . . I got a cab outside. Owe him a bit. Would you take care of the matter, dear?

NICA

How much, Bud?

BUD

A fifty will do nicely. And maybe that purple beret over there, this dude in the cab is a real French-lover, hey!

MONK

Bud!

NICA

It's okay, Thelonious. Make him feel at home. Be right back.
(Exits).

MONK

Of all the lousy, cheating, conniving, goddamn trickery.

BUD

I dig. Hey, man, now you know who you got here. Know I got that sweet tooth for luxury.

MONK

But you can't pay.

BUD

Somebody always does. Hey, now, what's up?

MONK

Remember, HORNIN' IN— well I got it now. Every kind of sax, trumpet, man, even trombone.

BUD

Hey.

MONK

Hey. But they sure know how to complicate it, though. Sometimes...
　　　(sees something in the distance)
I hear them yeah, screeching tires and all, the police, always hassling me, all that bull.
　　　(snaps back to BUD)
But, shit, band's best around, seems.

BUD

　　　(At first confused, then relieved.)
Hey, what? Some kind of a bitch, huh?

　　　(They laugh, pause).

MONK

It's good to see you, Bud. Looks like you caught it rough, though. Man, you back for good?

BUD

No, man. I just slipped away to see you.

MONK

Right.

BUD

There's been some people taking or I should say been trying to take care of me. Yeah, monitoring my every move and whatnot.

MONK

I can just imagine.

BUD

Hey!

MONK

They probably all dragged out by now. Sheeit.

BUD

Hey, you know it. PARISIAN THOROUGHFARE, you dig. Down this street, up that one, hey, where did Bud go?
(They laugh.)
But, serious, it's bad, see, whatever scratch I can make, it goes to them. Some kind of deal got worked out. These goons are like on the payroll. I didn't ask for them but there they are and all the rest of that jazza-matazz.

MONK

Yeah, good old THOROUGHFARE. I've been digging it for years. Least about ten or so. Always been a handful, always somebody on your

70

tail. When you're fucking around, it's a natural consequence. Sheeit. What's new, Bud?

BUD

Not much, man. Not a bit.

MONK

Your sound is kind of drunk, lately, man.

BUD

That's a style, Bud's choice.

(Hats get thrown back and forth during these exchanges, an air of rivalry is set.)

MONK

Hey, that's okay, man. Just don't have us fall off the stool with you. Why so lopsided in your sound?

BUD

It's all that's left. I've tasted them, the sweets of life. Too much. I've used them all up. Turned green from it all. Too much. The cream, the cherries, the sherry, butterscotch into scotch, caramel into rye. The bodacious, the curvaceous, the hellacious ones. Wildcats. Hellcats, too, if you get where I'm going. Left their marks all over me, man. Too much. Down the gullet until the sweetness dries your parched throat sore. Kills you, man. Music, too. Used up too many beautiful chords, embellishments, glissandoes, crescendoes. Hey, until I just couldn't breathe. Strangling, smothering, suffocating, couldn't think no more. Then the speed left me . . . with a passion only for the next bottle . . . nothing but a burning to get sauced. Left with only that, you dig? Then my sound turned funky-drunky, man.

MONK

Well, you certainly got it.

BUD

I've been true, Monk, to what we wanted to do.

MONK

Hey, that you have. Now what was that?

BUD

Quit jivin', man. Talking about the pact. I am my sound as much as you are yours, Monk. Hey, I listen and I can see all those institutions with the pea green walls. Feel those endless nights taking the guts right out of me. I get right back there. Alone and screeching through the night so fucking alone.

MONK

I know you've been expressing some extraordinary things.

BUD

Well, that's for you, my brother. So you know where I've been living. Right on the edge the whole time. Then when I get released they whisk me right to the damn studio, "Let's just get you down on record, Bud". With no discrimination, no taste, no vision. Just whatever came out at the moment. Sometimes I wasn't ready for that. Needed at least a hot bath, to get laid, whatever. No, just produce, like I might hang myself before they can get my tracks down. Hey, sometimes, man, I didn't even brush my teeth yet and there I'd be doing BUD ON BACH, CLEOP-ATRA'S DREAM. And where's my dreams? Sheeit.

MONK

Yeah, that's how they do us. Bud, you've been true to it. Need for you to know that. Here, you can wear this one,
    (throws him skullcap)
You're ordained now.

BUD

Alright I get it. Shuck that old cornpone, I dig.

MONK

Tiring me out with all that high and mighty jazz.

BUD

Yeah, me too. On the way down at twenty-one. What a mean break! Sheeit. Depending on others to keep me straight. Shit, hate that. Watching what I'm doing all the time. Pouring milkshakes down my throat so I don't drink the booze. Doing that monitoring, making jive out of my social life, queering my associations, like I'm a child away from that piano.

MONK

Well.

BUD

Maybe it's true but... I got one manly thing I got to do that nobody will take from me.

MONK

What are you driving at?

BUD

Hey, get this one, man. Some dog ran away with my shoes. Put me on a track right through Switzerland or Finland or some damn cold, cheesy land. Dig and all the hills start playing ROUND ABOUT SWITCH-KNIFE and out the door, I go. People running from me, can't stand it. Night and day. My soul's been damned and my body's been scorched with acid too many times for a body to endure. How many lives you think I got left? Eaten away by loneliness and one thought pounding my mind. Where, oh where's all my sweet friends? Over on the other side of the world. Goddamn separating ocean. Wish I could just hop it sometime.
(breaks up)
You know, Monk, man. Like a freight train. Right before the face in my ghoulish dreams takes me out of here, I told Frankie, he's my friend

in Paris. Hey, man, don't book me no more places, got to see my sweet friend Monk one last time. He's laid his life down for me, no, I didn't forget. Shock treatments made me forget them for a while but mind's back to remembering the important things. I know what you've done for me, Monk.

MONK

That's only because you was driving me crazy in that jail, Bud. And you are working back along those same lines right now.

BUD

No, man, it was something else. You did it, because it was me.

MONK

Hey!

(Nica enters).

NICA

I'll tell you, that guy outside is the rudest peasant I have ever spoken to. Asked me if I sleep with all musicians or only the black ones. He's lying in a pool of multiple feline fecundity right now. He's out of our hair for awhile. How about some cocoa and rum, Bud?

BUD

No, Lady Nica, no. Got to be sober here right now. Geez, Lady, ever think of becoming my bodyguard? Sheeit.

MONK

What? Did I hear right? Staying sober?

BUD

Hey, I know. It's unreal. But got to be, you'll see.

MONK

But on New Years Eve? Too much.

BUD

I best remember this one. Probably my last. Monk, how come you ain't with Nellie and the kids?

MONK

Never you mind. No. Look we'll talk later. After I play the gig. We'll have us an all-nighter like 1941, hey? Got to go cat-nap now with all the cats.

BUD

I don't see any. Who? Dizzy, Buster?

MONK

No, man, real ones. The kinds with four legs, dig? Nica's got about a hundred of them in the next room. She's stranger than you.

NICA

Or even you, Thelonious.

MONK

Or me. Or the moon, even.
　　(They laugh)
I'm going to fall out for half an hour.

NICA

Why don't you join him, Bud?

BUD

I'd like to go to the gig with you. Like to see all them society wags all nodding up and down to ROOTIE TOOTIE GONE SNOOTY. Hey!

MONK

Hey yourself. Watch out!

BUD

But see, I got a problem out there. Always one or the other. Always somebody hired to make me miserable. Nixing my attractions. Clipping any distractions. Living on my money, what precious little there is of it. Always got the same look. Wide brim hat, with snip eyes and a tippity-toes of a gumshoe walk.

MONK

Stay.

BUD

Alright. I'd like to take care of things here.

MONK

Just don't mess with too much over here.

BUD

You have a ball and all that jazz.

MONK

Yeah. Later.

BUD

Oh, one more thing I've got to ask you. Can you carry my coat 'til you reach the car. The tippity-toes, remember?

MONK

Shit. Anything else? How about a whole box of disguises? Helmets, caps, hats of a thousand mind-sets. On second thought, what the hell would fit yours, huh?

(As he falls out, he mentally works out with his ten piece band)
And a chorus of...Bebop was my flop. Understand? Not for the others.

They, well, see they kind of took off. Most of them fell flat after a while. Flat like dead or burnt out. They just about always took themselves out.

(To band.)

Another chorus of. . . yes. . . good. . . and like that. . .

(To Audience.)

out for good. For real.

(Band.)

And then you do like this... You can say they don't get around much . . . yeah . . . once more? Why not? Waited long enough. And once more . . . yeah, long time coming. Now? Today, it's like a magic carpet ride. 'cept for some shit that's clouding . . . no, never mind. No, not complaining, got no right. Man, today, like, everything is solid.

(Asleep)

(Lights fade, NICA is alone).

NICA

Fall light, both of you. You're tight as drums. You need to fall light. But in this world? It happens so seldom. Only the snow falls so light, that's all.

(She stares out window watching the snow fall.)

BLACKOUT

(After the concert. BUD has straightened the place up and prepared a big meal. He is dressed to the nines in MONK'S oversized clothes. His hair is spiffed up. He is in very high spirits and dances around room. MONK and NICA enter. MONK is tired. He nods to BUD).

NICA

Well, I'll be, what have you done to my place, Bud?

BUD

Me and the cats did some groomin' while you were gone. How did it
go, Monk?

MONK

Alright.
>(Looks around at BUD's handiwork and mutters to self)

Now, I'll have to leave here, too. Is there anywhere a man can go that
just lays like a rumpled bed?
>(Goes off on a tirade to unseen concert promoter.)

Goddamn spoiled uppity squares! Don't dig playing for them. Not at
all. Where's the people that follow me, huh? Where the hell are they?
Unsavory whippity-snips! Felt like I was playing some rinkety-dink
dive. Sheeit! Like '52. Some hick, jive lounge out on some moonshine
highway. Hey, man, I want better treatment next time, hear! Calling out
they want to touch my hat. Sheeit. Don't matter where it is you play.
Still treated like a plain, jivey piano player. Same as it's always been, no
different.

BUD

Hey man, it's not everyone I do my cooking and cleaning for. Should be
mighty grateful. Fact is, I've never done it before. Never know, could be
start of something big. Bigger than any of us might think. Bud's House
of Goodies, your after the concert cuisine. People showing up from
miles around dying to get a taste and you're here with that long face.
Man, I wore out my best apron for you.

NICA

Well, you've done a great job, Bud. Monk, sit down and eat this fabu-
lous meal Bud has prepared.

MONK

Gotta hit the wind for a bit, get some air. Too tight in here.
>(Exits.)

NICA

Let me explain some things to you, Bud. Thelonious has not quite been himself lately.

BUD

What in the shit's got into him? Never seen him this way. That's for sure.

NICA

It would be better if I let you see for yourself or if Thelonious discusses it with you when he is ready. The main thing with him that I have noticed is his hallucinations.

BUD

Hallucinations, huh?

NICA

Yes. At least that is what my doctor friends have termed it.

BUD

What in the hell is he doing the hallucinating about?

NICA

Ssh. He's coming back.

MONK

(Oblivious to BUD and NICA. Punctuating his words, he spins, twists and turns his body into a state of frenzy until he snaps back to reality.)

You know what it's like? Checking your friends out going ahead and whooping it up while you're outside rustling the bread to pay to get in to see them play. Got a gig for me, you say? In Carolina. Do I get to come back alive? Play it safe, you mean nothing original. I see, well, what is it you want? I Got Rhythm? How about I leave out the fucking beat? Maybe you want an organ grinder instead? Thought you might have caught my name with an "e" after it? Sheeit. Bud, what're you doing here? Suppose to be in Paris, aren't you? How did I do tonight, Nica?

NICA

Sublime, Thelonious.

BUD

Did you do TOOTIE? MONK'S MOOD?
(MONK nods)
Was Nellie and the kids there ?

MONK

What the hell is this sudden preoccupation with my goddamn family, Bud? You some kind of social worker?

BUD

Hey, Monk, just asking, that's all.

MONK

Nowadays, everybody's some kind of social worker. Can't just lay up in your bed away from it all. They all want to know you sleeping where? What's going on with you and yours? I can't just live and dig. I earned it, Bud. You're crazier than a coot and now you're calling the kettle black. Where's yours? Huh? Which wife are you on now? Which damn fool you've got hanging with you?

BUD

Got no one, just my friend Frank.

MONK

Frank! Seems a bit queer.

BUD

No, it's not like that.

MONK

Hey, man, I don't care. That's my point. And should be yours. There's nothing wrong with wanting to stay away. I stayed when easiest thing would've been to split but I did my best to be concerned with all and whatnot with the kids and Nellie and all their carrying ons when all I wanted was to phase everything right out. Know what I mean? Now, man, they can be better off and more comfortable but I need some peace. Phones ringing and stuff. How can I create? Concentrate on any damn thing? Huh? Tell me?

BUD

I dig you, man. Don't need to get all hostile. I dig it.

MONK

Then do that, do! Man, you didn't answer my first question. Now, what are you doing here?
(Agitated, he starts heading for door again.)
Never understood it. How the hell are they booking all the pupils in the clubs and not the teacher. I know, it's no mystery. Everybody's got that old cabaret card but me.
(Wheels around to BUD.)
And on account of the Tombs, 1951 and you!
(points at NICA)
We're talking 'round about '59. Flying through the night on pills and booze in a silver Bentley. Goofing and ragging on those tippity-toes dying to catch what they call me, "that dangerous, big mother". Well, they did and I lose that damn card again. Hey, I'm talking here.

NICA

Thelonious, now get back to tonight. You had two wonderful sets tonight and everyone dug you.

MONK

Bull.

BUD

Hey! Hey! Hey! Get with it! Which world are you in, man? The lady's trying to reach you, man. And me, too. Now listen, whatever's doing this let's have it right now. I'm not going to be here again and I knew you're in trouble so here I am.

MONK

(Eyeing the window, he anxiously paces and physically withdraws, isolating himself from the others, trying to insulate himself within himself, the room, whatever feels safe and continues this process throughout following speeches regarding his inner turmoil.)

False move here, false one there. Man, you wind up on the garbage heap. Don't take much. Bars, like prison bars can be built up in a hurry and brought on by all kinds of things. A slight in the past that you swallowed and thought you put it away. Or a loss of dignity where you thought you understood something and had made peace with it comes back and kicks you just as you're getting up on that stage. Right when they announce your name and people are clapping and you start re-membering. Reliving it all. Shit. Or when you're taking a bath or eating a piece of meat in your kitchen and you scream out at your wife and wonder why and shit. Then it comes. You know and you wish it'd finally stop but it's just starting. Right? Bud, I'm asking.

BUD

(Reliving his own private hell along with MONK, can only repeat.)

Yeah. And you wish it was ending but you know it's just starting.

(goes catatonic.)

MONK

(grabs a piece of bread from table, chews in BUD's face.)

Didn't I just say that? Hey, Bud!

BUD

Quit your yelling. I can hear you.

MONK

Then look alive!

BUD

Isn't so simple. A shiver's running through me. Nica?

NICA

Goddamnit! Listen to each other. And don't look at me to solve anything. I can't figure out any of my own business. I'm not even an artist,
I'm just a renegade. I don't get weighed down. One of my cardinal rules.
Hey, you know something? Try juggling four or five lovers at one time
and holding onto your sanity and retaining your sensitivity as a person.
That can get pretty hairy, I'll tell you. You guys just have to get the notes
to work out. I'm lucky half the time to escape with my body parts left
in good working order.

BUD

Sorry, Lady. Sorry, I asked.

NICA

I know, I'm hip and cool and heavily educated. Suave, enchanting and
with enough savoir faire to run a hipsters' carnival but this you're both
going to have to work out. Thelonious, how about some cigars to cele-
brate the New Year?

MONK

We're out, baby.

NICA

Oh shit. And I was so in the mood for one. How about you?

MONK

Yeah. Bud?

BUD

Yeah.

NICA

I'll go and get them.
>   (She goes to the door, "Happy New Year" is heard from the outside
>   and then a car horn. Scene gets more intense inside.)

BUD

Monk, man, you've changed.

MONK

Can't be a rock forever.

BUD

Monk, I'm scared. Feels like you're getting what I got?

MONK

Maybe so. What's it feel like?

BUD

Man, have you been putting me on? I mean, what's with the spinning
act?

MONK

Wigging out to survive. Been doing it for years, Bud.

BUD

Well, it certainly wigged me out good. What's the goof?

MONK

No goof, though. Crazy people are left alone.

BUD

(Does crazy gyrations.)

Like this?

MONK

Now just keep still. Every time another door slammed, another mother walked away taking something I taught and made a bundle for himself and somebody behind him, I felt them bars. Every time I sent my wife to do a man's job and earn some bread for the kids I shut myself down. Clamped tight. I shut my eyes and my ears to what was around me and concentrated to the max on what I know I was put here to do. Price being paid now for that, you can be sure. Dig what I say, Bud?

BUD

Sure thing, Monk. But all that is over now. You got it made. Can sit back and take it all in now.

MONK

Just not natural to me.

BUD

What are you feeling about that?

MONK

What do I feel 'bout what? Hey, man, get out of here. Sounding phony with all that fiddling around.

BUD

What? I don't read you?

MONK

What are you trying to come off as, huh? A watchamacallsit? A shrink.

BUD

Man, don't get so drug. Just trying to help out, anyway. Using what it is I know something about. Had me some practical exposure to the species, might say.

MONK

I've been at one of those hospitals, you know! They let me out without any hullabaloo.

BUD

Let me out of a few too. Don't prove nothing.

MONK

Well, just keep it quiet.

BUD

(As the scene gets more tense, BUD starts to incessantly comb his hair, more and more violently and obsessive.)

Yessir.

MONK

Can't bullshit you.

BUD

No, you can't. So why try?

(Silence).

MONK

I've seen some things. Some frightening, ghoulish things. Been like shadows.

BUD

Shadows in the night?

MONK

In the night, in the day. All the fucking time. No drug, no drink will quiet them. Only makes them worse.

BUD

Comes with the territory.

MONK

Different stuff.

BUD

Oh?

MONK

Yeah.

> (Silence, music plays as MONK falls into trance and speaks from deep in his soul, his life, BUD's life passing through his being as he makes connections between them. The section in quotes notates a process of compositional creation forming in his mind as the music plays along with the speech. MONK is more animated in unison with the music during this section. BUD recognizes the creation taking place.)

Dissonances of incidence. Coincidence. We've been pulled together, for all time. Linked forever. On our own and jointly. We had a notion of a sound a long time ago and we promised to be true to it. And to each other, too. Dig! I know you do. Yeah, now especially. We've been apart. Life sometimes. Intrusions, distractions, clashes, by necessity, too. We were long distance but the messages kept travelling. Like this, I hear a sound behind a sound, making a fluffy romance become the blues. A space, a pause dying to be filled but waiting for just the right moment. My gloom got so deep, took me over, I knew you were feeling it, too. Yeah, the blues, no rescue, it's so bottomless, so pure. When I look into your eyes, Bud, I know there is no cure. See, Bud, lots of pain makes up a man's music and it pops up all over his stuff. But love also. The main thing is, how alive he is, how alive the music is. A man and his music.

It's all the same, dig? Gets in and fires his sound and when that sound gets brought down to a whimper, it's time for some questions to be asked. Hard ones. Time to look out for each other. Now, sit, old friend and look at me, Bud. Tell me true, can I still reach for it and come on back to reality? I don't know. What do you see? I can't see anything now. I'm dependent on you like in '46 when you recorded my sheets for the first time and I couldn't rustle up a dime. I'll never forget it. Never. All the cats went their own way— Bird, Diz and Klook, but we fixed our points together for good. For awhile, your hands spread my music and I lay home with my hopes in a bucket, then you gave out. I kept going 'til they finally saw what it is all along. Always shown that you see, Bud. Nobody can play my sound except me and you. You always could play my insides out, whatever you were feeling. And now maybe my insides turned out. You understand? Dissonance/ Incidence/ Discord/ Coincidence. Hope to hell, I can still heal.

(As speech ends, MONK's energy dissipates with the creative
energy and internal pain spent. A sheet of music now lays at his feet.
He goes silent and is only barely present until NICA's outburst.)

BUD

(Acknowledging the creation and the effort. BUD is in awe of
MONK's honesty and genius but then grows insecure and anxious
as the silence haunts him.)

Masterpiece, man. I never quit, man. Never, you hear. Even when I couldn't do those fancy things anymore. I put it in another direction. Mainly 'cause of you. I knew you were locked up at home, never working on the outside but always knicking away at some damn tune. Started putting down what I was feeling even if I couldn't do those Bud Powell runs anymore. Brakes were on, but they stuck. Lifetime wasn't enough to get better from the beatings, no! Slide down, can't adjust to . . . out on a limb, where I've got to be all the time but can't from hospital beds, rooms with glass cages, stop brakes on! Walls with wires, fields of electricity clamp, cramp the style, scream's the same as a kiss where I'm from, same. Clashing streams of sounds on outer edges of, of, of elastic foam, trying to reach the rubber part where it bounces back.

Breathing can be difficult and thinking is sure weird. Hands and fingers don't correspond with the mind anymore, lost the exact point, points, exactly, understand. Where we all came in, none of it, so. Like you always said- search for your own thing, no matter what else is going on—

(He is interrupted by a frantic NICA entering out of breath.)

NICA

Good news and bad news, guys. Bud, you now have two new friends outside and they are getting restless. Sorry, Monk, had to give them the booze and cigars to buy time.

(Lights dim inside and searchlights throw off glare on windows.
Men slump down, protectively and play possum. They use this
as a reflex defense mechanism to ward off forces attempting to
incarcerate them. NICA speaks in haze).

I will let you both in on a little lie. I am not as indestructible as I appear to be. Yes, I am fluent in six, no seven languages as well as the bop idiom. Surrounded by my beloved jazz musicians, I curse the stench of conformity. I fly furiously in the face of my ancestral lineage and all that polluted jazz. Europeans! And royal ones! What a stifling and cursed pain in the arse, n'estce pas? Need I say more about where I'm from? My old schoolmates and childhood comrades gossip and mock me as I pierce them to the core with sullen hatred. Of course, I am usually having too much fun living up to my outrageous reputation. In my youth, I would ride bareback on a horse, not the horse bare, but me, during the annual hunt. How dare they make sport of animals! Those hypocritical, high-browed bestial old figs. I defy them all! I was so lonely there as a young girl. I dared to live in a dream of special people and places of my choosing. A dream where individuality and daring would be taken for granted. A place where a superior intellect would be applauded. Where wit and humor is the crowning jewel. Thelonious, Bud, I can honestly say that I have never been happier than right now. Thelonious, Bud! What the hell's happened here?

(MEN stare straight out, NICA spots new sheet of music, BUD
smiles up at her, catatonic but with a look of grace on his face.

NICA runs to window picks up poker from fireplace and strafes windows. MEN jolt to consciousness.)
I spit on the damn authorities everywhere—you've done enough— and seek the wind— new horizons, where a newborn idea can take flight safely, securely —
(The MEN gently take hold of her.)
We're safe inside, don't worry. Watch out for glass.

BLACKOUT

END OF ACT I

ACT II

(Lights up. BUD and NICA are onstage. Both are exhausted. It
is two hours later. Windows are damaged from NICA's outburst.
They are wearing coats. There are sounds of cats caterwauling in the
distance, intermittently broken by the sound of MONK agitatedly
discoursing to himself outside the window. His shadow looms eerily
through shattered window, a jagged presence as dawn is breaking.)

BUD

Dig feeding these cats. Could get used to staying here, Nica. What do
you say 'bout that?

NICA

What can one say? What, dear didn't exactly hear you?

BUD

Talking 'bout staying. Setting up shop here. Last hurrah and all, what
say, Nica darling? What say?

MONK

(From outside as he paces.)

Billie Holiday! Hey! Billie! Hey, now! Billie Holiday! You could save
my ass! Nellie Smith! Nellie Monk, don't want me, no more. No. Billie!
Used to stare up at the ceiling, had your picture smiling, crying, whin-
ing at me. Oh, Billie. Red lights ringed 'round your face. Inspiring me.
Nellie, my Nellie, can't survive without you. But don't want to hurt you
darling. Can't be tinkering at home no more. Told me no more pain
'round kids, baby. Gone, Gone. Love. Inspiration. Need it. Gone. Nellie.
Gone. Billie. Got to move. Not safe 'round here. No longer.

BUD

Going on all night. What are we going to do? He can't be carrying on through morning.

NICA

Yes, Bud. He can carry on forever, I let him down. Stopped the quiet. Stopped the safety, the peace. I failed.

BUD

No, Lady, never. You kept the man floating through all the years. Kept clothes on his back and his family's back. Don't blame yourself for —

NICA

Will he just roam and roam out there? What has been unleashed inside of him now? Scars that are so undying.

BUD

Let me try, baby. I'll make him step out of himself.
        (Out window.)
Hey there, Monk. How's the old chill? I said, how's the old Hudson holding up?
        (Pause.)
Made friends with my cronies out there, huh? Man, you driving us bat-ty in here. It 's creepy, you big old bear wearing out the riverbank, want to put us in the middle of some heavy water? Man, haven't we paid enough dues? Especially this fine lady here. Saved your ass 'bout a hun-dred times, as I figure it. You know, patron saints don't grow on trees. And I know it isn't for your old ugly face, she lay it all on the line, hey!

NICA

It's no use. Has to run its course. Soon he'll focus.

BUD

What?

NICA

You must understand that when Thelonious has something new down
on paper
> (picks up music sheet)

he immediately has to try it out.
> (BUD looks at her puzzled.)

One of the advantages of his-

MONK

Where's safe? What's safe? What? What?

BUD

Lady, we've got to do something. Call Nellie.

NICA

No, the appropriate call is to the dawn jam at Coleman Hawkins' place.

BUD

Still got his spot on the park?

NICA

The same.

MONK

Nellie! Billie! Nellie? Billie?
> (Coming through the door, rising, growing in size, stature as
> purpose starts to form.)

Out of my way. Need some room. Something's beginning to march on
in my head. New and big and spreading into wide directions. Making
me lose where I am. About to break on free from the safety. Don't need
to be dragged down no more with that. Hear!

BUD

Good to see you back, man. Hey, now-

(A long, ominous silence ensues. BUD finally flinches and breaks across room. MONK catches him and shakes him. NICA shrinks back, amazed.)

MONK

You know, Bud, seeing you this night stayed up in my mind over at the concert. Wasn't thinking 'bout what I 'm doing up there, only 'bout August, 1951, the year of the Tombs, man. Our year of the Tombs.

BUD

Knew it, man. Knew you'd get to it. It came back to me this year, Monk.

MONK

Funny thing, man. Start to occupy me this here night. Hadn't thought 'bout it in a helluva long time. Must've been you coming 'round tonight, Bud.

BUD

I can see that. Don't have to explain it. I can understand—

MONK

No, you don't understand, man. Don't have a jumping clue. Don't know nothing 'bout it. Just got a lot of feeling or you think you've got a lot of feeling on it. Don't have nothing, man. You just went and suckered me, too. Don't exactly see how but I'll get to it, man.

BUD

Hey, now —

NICA

Thelonious, that does appear to be unfair.

MONK

Oh, yeah. Well, let's see how it comes out when I develop what had happened there. Got two guys on the street. One, who's me, doesn't have anywhere to be on this street except his friend is wailing away that he can't stay in life natural and has to have something to fix his head this particular night. I say, man, I've got to get upstairs and tend to what I have to do. Besides, Nellie will not share your kind of view and I better not be 'round you. So, I'm trying to get out.

BUD

It's true, I don't let him go up.

NICA

Still, I don't see where it's leading to Bud's manipulating you-

MONK

And you won't the way you're breaking in to my telling of this story. So. . . up and out I try to go when old Bud here lays on the shit thick as a Tatum crescendo. "Monk, I'm a goner 'less you stick out this night with me. I've got it bad tonight. Losing a lot of things lately". (They return to scene as it happened.)

BUD

. . . lately, man. My pad's just 'bout gone and they're talking 'bout holding my piano.

MONK

Where'd the bread go, Bud?

BUD

Everywhere it wasn't supposed to. But I have to get through it, man. Have to keep the driving fear, the awful shaking fact that I'm not standing up by myself away, man. Got to keep it all down, dig? Sure, you do, man, sure you do. Monk understand, man, don't I know.

MONK

Well, Bud, Monk's going to walk away from you, man. Nellie says I have too many of my own ghosts, own blues in the closet and she doesn't mean the song, man. It's real, Bud. You know 'bout real, man? That's when the kids are screaming for food and milk, man. And all their eyes are looking your way. Got your hands down at your sides and your head down to the floor. That's when you're dying to play a gig somewhere, anywhere, man. And you've got no prospects for that and yet you've got so much damn music busting out of your heart, your soul, you're splitting apart from the hunger and you're dying from losing hope. What do you know 'bout real, man? That's real, baby.

BUD

Just stay 'til I cop the shit, man. Do that much for me, man, please.

MONK

This deal better happen soon enough, Bud.

BUD

Here they come.

BLACKOUT

(Lights up minutes later. BUD is very high on heroin. MONK is wary and uncomfortable.)

BUD

Way out.

MONK

Great.

BUD

What you moping 'bout? I offered you some of that shit, didn't I? Well?

MONK

This is where I get off, man. Going upstairs, just get on your way, man. See you tomorrow—

BUD

What you mean? Hey, man. Get on back here. Oh man, I've got to come right out with it, now.

MONK

Out with what?

BUD

Have you been working? I'll answer. No, right?

MONK

What's it to you?

BUD

Well, maybe I can help along those lines.

MONK

So, out with it.

BUD

I have an idea but you've got to hang with me for a while.

MONK

It's going to take more than that to keep my interest, Bud.

BUD

Alright, here's the deal. Keep me company, Monk. Watch out for Bud all the way and I'll do this for your skinny career. You go travelling with Bud. I make a pitch to the label. You ready for this? The Bud and Monk Show. Dynamite Duets of Bop. Unbelievable virtuosity in contrasts. Creation in motion for all the world to see. The master and the maestro. It will be like The Duke and the Count. The Prez and Hawk. Dueling and wailing like out of this world. My name and your tunes. Our tunes. When they laugh at your comical inventions I'll slay them with my dexterity. Maybe we can hook up with Dexter while we're at it. What say, Monk? Some gas, hey?

MONK

Could work, I suppose. You say you got some backing?

BLACKOUT

(Lights up. The MEN are confined now. There is a sound heard throughout of men moaning and wailing in desperation.)

MONK

Goddamn it, Bud, busted. Now, we're in for it.

BUD

Now, you're in for it. I'm getting out, man. I've got to. You need to help me, man. I won't be able to take it in here.

MONK

And what 'bout me? What makes you so different than me, huh?

BUD

This. Hear those sounds. I'm going to make some sounds that the buzzards are going to run from. Man, I have been in the hell-holes and I can't pay any more of those dues, dig? Dig? Not the great Bud Powell. Been beaten 'round here (indicates his head.) Once, no, 'bout a hundred too many times. Hey, ofays! Hey, motherfuckers! Yeah, all y'all.

MONK

Ssh! What the hell you trying to do, Bud? Already got us busted claiming that we are the second musical coming of Moses and Aaron. Now I'm convinced you are trying to get us killed.

BUD

Hey, yourself! Sheeit! Ain't spending any more time fucking 'round here. Hey, you hear! You breathing the same goddamned air as the greatest piano player God ever made! How dare you look on me with such contempt, you out there! Yeah, all of you! Only I got the stuff to have this kind of pride hear! I should be out there and you all should be cooped up in here, right, Monk? What 'bout it, Monk?

(tones voice down and pleads with MONK.)

I'll break, man. Right in two. Need you to show me something, man, I couldn't ask my own brother for. Got to get me out of here. OUT THE FUCK OUTTA HERE OR I'LL YELL 'TIL ALL THESE OTHER VOICES DROWN! I PROMISE! BUD KEEPS HIS PROMISE! EVER HEAR A CRAZY MAN YELL? MONK? MONK?

(MONK puts hand over BUD's mouth.)

MONK

That's it, there's no reason for two to die. Get this man a doctor! He's not responsible, I did it. Need somebody? Well, here I am. Let this man out, please. I'm your criminal.

(As lights fade to black.)

I'm the dog, I can growl. God gave me a growl to save my ass. God gave me a back to bear the pain. I'll steel myself to do what I'm obviously called upon to do here. But please, God, please whatever's, whomever's up there, don't whip my growl for good.

(Lights up. We are back into the present. MONK has BUD in his grasp again.)

BUD

Yeah, it happened like that. I'm not very proud.

NICA

Oh, Bud, Thelonious doesn't condemn you for it.

MONK

Yeah it's alright to understand him. But hear this, what's stuck deep in my craw this night. I never got free so easy. Everybody thinks, sure, Monk can take it. He has a strong back. He's seen lots of failure. Plenty of rejection, dejection, whatnot. But keep this in mind, too. 'Cause

I did for a long while. My life changed completely since that night. And I crawl in August since then. I, Thelonious Monk skulks way into the night in August. You know that? Well, you should. Something got broken. What nobody knows is that I haven't made music since what I had going up to 1951. What are you looking at? It's true. Believe it. Where I was going, who knows? I was on the verge of some damn kind of miraculous breakthrough, too. Who knows? It set me back to a place, you don't come back from.

BUD

Now, man, I can't believe what I'm hearing. You're making crazy talk. You've beaten that kind of pressure a million times in your life. You've got the output to show for that, man. Don't you know it?

MONK

No, man, I don't know it. And what the hell do you know 'bout it? What do you know what was in my head in 1951? Huh? You think I'm some sort of cowboy, some sort of John Wayne? Ride out a place like that, just like nothing happened to me? You came in a boy when I first met you and stole the people following me back in '41 in Minton's after I gave you a break. What do you know? I fell flat there after you left. What do you know? I had lots of projects, lots of plans in '51. I was right there with as much in my head as Ellington had. That's right. I used most of it lulling myself to quiet the nerves, ignoring the pain all 'round I saw, I felt, they all felt, all those men inside there. Saving myself in that menagerie for humans. I was hoarse from playing all the ideas I had inside of me and working them out through my throat. When I got out of there, I didn't look back. 'Til now, that is. That's how it was after I hung with you and some of the joy I used to have got lost. It went down the drain out of those fucking shit pans they gave us in those Tombs, man.

(Grabs BUD.)

I'm an artist, man! Like you, maybe more. Not some goddamn hero cowboy from no movie. Don't even watch movies, man. Yeah, it was good copy later. Yeah, maybe Nica, too, was drawn to me from hearing 'bout what I did for you, my buddy. My good, conning buddy. But wasn't true. Broke me. I turned in my growl. Lost my special one. Become a "mercy me" growl instead of "turning world upside down" growl. Which I started with and goddamn Bud-you know all about it.

BUD

Hey, I know about loss, Monk.

MONK

What do you know? Wise up, man. You always had it made. You threw it away, Bud. As sick as you were, you still tossed it, man. What do you know 'bout standing 'round watching others steal your sound, your bread, your spark. You know what I'm talking 'bout? No, you don't. You were always provided for soon as you recover. Me, I stared up at a wall, stood outside a gate and felt the icy chill of my brothers' mockery, effrontery as they went on by. Bud, my humor died in the Tombs. For you, baby, it was just another temporary address.

BUD

Shit, Monk. I didn't know. I love you, man.

NICA

Thelonious, breathe deep. Thelonious, relax, relax just for a moment right now.

MONK

He loves me. Well, what am I going to do with that?

BUD

I'll tell you, man. You listen, that's what 'cause it cuts both ways. Yeah, I leaned on you. Had to. But, man, the justice is yours. Today. Look 'round. Catch your own act, man. You've got your own prison made up now and I want you to break out. That's what I want. That's why I'm here. You've got more to say and the wherewithal to say it. Hey, I also gave you a gift from back then. If it brought you this fine lady-you've got nothing to complain 'bout, anyway. Maybe you're not Ellington but you're a monster yourself and you've given me more years to live, 'cause Monk, man, I guarantee you, I would've died surely in that cage. I tell you from the bottom of my lying, thieving soul. There wouldn't have been no more Bud and no more long distance communications between your brother here and your humorless self. You would've lost more than a few jokes.

MONK

Yeah, alright. So, how do we go 'bout getting out of this jam-up?

BUD

Well, I guess there's a few things wouldn't hurt for me to find out 'bout how Lady N here, how much she played a part in all of that. Maybe that will put you in a more charitable mood.

NICA

Thelonious and I go back to the time of the bust. I read about this extraordinary action taken on account of need. Yours, Bud. And I resolved to befriend the great man who could give himself up for his brother.

MONK

No! Saved two by saving one, that's all.

(Back in time to 1951 where NICA and MONK meet on a dark street.)

MONK

You the lady I been hearing 'bout saved my time in that jail through someone knowing somebody hocus—pocus?

NICA

I rather be the one known for getting the work of one special person out to a wide audience. If you can hack it, that is.

MONK

Could be alright with me. How does one address you, my lady?

NICA

Same as anyone else. "Hey, you", will suffice, if the situation calls for it.

MONK

Crazy.

NICA

Blue.

MONK

Could be, if one is walking that way at night.

NICA

I only walk alone at night.

MONK

You dig me fine.

NICA

Quietly, Thelonious, take my arm, let's stroll.

MONK

(As they begin to walk.)
Has Bud been taken care of?

NICA

He's in the best institution again.

MONK

Got that room with the chords on the wall reserved for him by now. Ought to name the place for him. Ought to be a way clear for him to live out his time in peace, where he can't do all that acting up.

NICA

Heard a visa's been prepared.

MONK

Feel it's more than something you've heard. Maybe something you and
Nellie arranged.

NICA

Possibly.

MONK

Say no more. Just before you met me here I was following a beam of
light in the sky. Took me 'bout thirty blocks out of the way. Saw something in that part of the sky that I've never felt before. Told me something will happen in a while.

NICA

Yes, I saw it, too. It stood out like a comet yet no one acted as if anything strange was happening. Why is that you suppose?

MONK

You think Bud will be all right over the ocean?

NICA

I don't know but I'm sure he will do all he can to come back. I hope,
Thelonious, that you are ready for what will happen to your life. Your
life will be special.

MONK

Couldn't be more than it's been. Got that one lady in my heart and now
I know you've come in my life for something to happen. I didn't do all
I've done for no one to hear what I've got to say. In the Tombs, there
were some who spent their whole life that way. Shouting at a blank wall.
I know that isn't my purpose in life. I like you, lady. I think you know
what I've been talking 'bout. I think that we're on a moon of a different

making than the rest. You know I'm making the greatest music right now I ever made and I do not know if I'll be playing in public again.

NICA

Perhaps not today nor in the near future but immortality wears a baffling disguise.

MONK

Yes. I got to get to the far future.

(They share a laugh.)

(Lights out and come back on to present. MONK strides through room with purpose.)

MONK

Open territory. I'm forty-six years old, even though I feel like I'm sixty. Like Bird. Like Christian, shit. Like all of them at this point. This same point.

BUD

I dig you.

MONK

Bring it all on! I can handle the invention. This is my most adventurous time ever. You'll see. Hold on, let it come! Hold on, hear the echo. Play those ruts and angles. I'll do it like only I'm born to do. See!

NICA

Clearly, Thelonious.

MONK

Good.

BUD

Hey!

MONK

Yeah.

NICA

Thelonious, about before.

MONK

Forget it. You are the most, baby. Where'd I be without you?

NICA

Much better off, I dare say.

BUD

I think this lady's on mud pills.

NICA

Mud pills?

MONK

(Playing along.)
Sure, I heard of them. Everything incredibly bad happens to everybody else 'cause of you.

NICA

Oh, no.

BUD

Oh, yeah.

MONK

Nica, gas it up! Gas up the old Bentley. We're taking a ride to Hawk's. Before it fades.

NICA

Righto, let me get the number.

MONK

And pack up some bags. We're getting out of here for awhile.

BUD

Wait. I like it here. I mean, I'll go anywhere you all are travelling. I mean, I—

MONK

Shit. Can't carry you, Bud.

BUD

What do you mean, man?

MONK

What I said, there's no mystery.

BUD

But you need me.

MONK

I do?

BUD

You do. I have saved you from your poor self tonight.

MONK

What? Are you crazy?

BUD

What do you think?

MONK

Man, c'mon. I know you are.

BUD

Well, guess again, buddy. Your time surely isn't long. You might stay on this planet physically a while longer, but the rest, shit.

MONK

What are you saying?

BUD

Man, you're in no better shape upstairs than me.

MONK

Prove it.

BUD

I can. Take me with you. Make a tour. Bud and Monk. Okay, Monk and Bud. Don't care, alright you're the name right now. Two greats for the price of one. We'll do only your tunes. Your straight ass way, my funky-drunky style. But all Monk compositions. What say?

MONK

Got possibilities. Yeah. What a scene! I like it. Nica!

NICA

Party's in full swing over at Hawk's. Any time you're ready.

MONK

What do you think 'bout the Monk and Bud Tour? Goddamn! Know it's insane but imagine...

NICA

I don't know, Thelonious. . . Let's give it some thought.

BUD

I don't have the time for waiting 'round.

NICA

But Bud, Thelonious is at a juncture in his career where all decisions must be weighed heavily.

BUD

I don't care! Running out of time. Need answers, need another moth-erfucking break and one from my friend. It's not science, not rhyme, it's just Philly, billy club, clubs, all of them. Monk, trains, train stations and holding head, Mother holds my hurt head all night like only a mother can do, understand. Brakes on! If only I did! Life gone, sound gone Monk gone from me, too long. Trails go cold! Only twenty-one! DAMN! The bond gets tight. Brakes on, if only, flame was bright, if only. Friend owes me, forever, sorry, if only I put those damn brakes on and think what I'm doing. Upon a time, this one that one so many others same thing comes back to me, to this head that never worked right away from all that music.

MONK

Stop this shit! Call Harry, my manager, Bud. He'll know what to do.

BUD

(Running to window calling out in a last desperate move, to save MONK, to save himself.)
BILLIE! NELLIE! Save him! Inspire him! Love him! BILLIE HOL-IDAY! NELLIE SMITH! NELLIE MONK! Red lights rung 'round ceiling, blowing hot, whistling cold caresses of genius 'round my man's pure solid soul of originality! And me, too. Me, too. No matter what's happened to me, to him.
(Collapses in great coughing jag.)

MONK

Nica? What about it?

                         NICA

You know the answer.

                         MONK

No, I don't. I really don't.

                         NICA

You great big child. Wonderful, innocent children. Neither of you see.

                         BUD

I see. I see.
          (Fades out in exhaustion.)
Told you that you're crazy, Monk. I knew it, Monk. Crazy me, crazy
you.

                         NICA

Let's make our move, Thelonious. We need to get going. Help Bud up.

                         MONK
          (As they head towards door.)
Baby, don't you know he's one step ahead of them tippity toes? He's in
another county, state, by now.

          (BUD sleeps.)

                         NICA

Of course.

          BLACKOUT

          (Lights up. MONK is alone still in NICA's house. He clutches
          sheet music as every now and then, he tries on different hats in
          preparation for going out. He can use this action to differentiate
          who's speaking.)

MONK

Bud, in your day, you played like the forces of nature untamed. A mighty howl of fired fancy you gave us but when you flame right on out I've got to confess I got scared for us all.

(There is a pause. MONK resumes as BUD.)

Monk, how come you never play any of my tunes?

(As MONK again.)

Only know one player for them. You.

(As BUD.)

Am I to take that as a no on the future or are you planning to make me a counter-offer?

(As MONK again.)

A man can only be himself, Bud.

(As BUD.)

So true, so true.

(As MONK again.)

What'll happen, Bud?

(BUD)

'Bout what?

(MONK)

When it comes, man. You've been through it.

(BUD)

Hold on as long as you can. When it plays out, get lost, disappear and leave yours a pot of gold.

(MONK)

Don't understand all these sideways back, man.

(BUD)

Too much, too many years. They all laughed at you, your own kind, the musicians. And you laughed back in the face of a cold, indifferent wind, years upon years in your room, poking, hammering and tooling away on some damn tune or another 'til they all added up and wham! Nobody could ignore Monk anymore. But, added up to too much 'round about now. Makes me feel like getting under a table seeing what you're going through, Monk.

(MONK)
That's 'bout how we feel it that close in each other, buddy.

BUD

(Appearing through window, head turned back over shoulder, as he
moves away.)
Hey, tell me again, Monk, 'bout my playing. To carry me back overseas
and ease the pain.

MONK

(As MONK begins speaking, NICA enters and goes to phone and
starts making calls. MONK gets a total resurgence of energy and
dances by himself to his thoughts and BUD's music.)
Never knew as pure a player as you. Thinking in three, four times a
man's natural thought. All music, man, just flowing and flowing. When
I saw you getting beat and losing your timing, I fell into some darkness,
so sad, just so I could hang on...
You sat down and it was like a hurricane, tornado and a flood all at
once. A mighty river rushing through. And I could feel life at its zenith.
I'd be living a dream when hearing a boy playing and feeling as deep as
a weathered old man could feel. That's my Bud always and will always
be Bud to the world.
(BUD exits and MONK falls out in a seated position, finally
content).

NICA

The roosters are crowing, the cats have finally shut up and the milkman
is coming up the drive. (Reaches through the doorway and presents
items). And finally without further adieu and with absolutely no dis-
cussion on how one slick lady managed to secure them. Cigars and
brandy for all! (She discovers that she is alone with the audience.) Now,
you might ask me was this a true meeting or a meeting only in the
cosmos? Well, I submit it happened but only if you are tuned into the
right frequency. A true friend will walk through a tornado even on
his last legs if he is summoned. When you see a brave hero who never

cracked in front of you, well, what you don't know, is…did he ever have to make that last crucial call? Did he ever howl into a blinding blizzard and discover enough of the sun's warmth to carry on? When one is eternally searching for a cradle to rest his weary head on, perhaps, in an instant, the unlikeliest source might materialize. Yes, just possibly… with just the most appropriate words to bring a little solace, a little sleep, a moment of renewal and… on we go to the next party, gathering, the next project never letting on that we are anything but the coolest, most indestructible beings on Earth. Yes, we have survived with our emotions intact. Naturally, no past confusion appearing on the surface only life in its glorious, wildly clear present. Ready to resume. Prepared to fly into the teeth of whatever comes our way. You hear? Good. C'est tout, my friends. All my friends.

BLACKOUT

END OF PLAY

Glenn Laszlo Weiss in TALES OF A JEWISH AMERICAN PRINCE
Photo Credit: Paul Mones

TALES OF
A JEWISH
AMERICAN
PRINCE

GLENN LASZLO WEISS

Note on
TALES OF A JEWISH AMERICAN PRINCE

TALES OF A JEWISH AMERICAN PRINCE runs between 90 and 100 minutes, though it is around 30 pages in text. This is because of the current music choices behind the pieces. By "pieces", I mean, for example, OUR SOUND or JEWS IN HEAVEN. SECOND GENERATION is the only piece without music and is done as a spoken rap. In TALES OF A JEWISH AMERICAN PRINCE, there is no singing intended but at certain moments, voices can undoubtedly be lifted, if felt. If an intermission is designated, it would make the most sense after Part Two. Part Three is about as long and Parts One and Two together.

TALES OF A JEWISH AMERICAN PRINCE was inspired by the New Jewish Music Scene of the 1990's in New York City and in some other parts of the world to a lesser degree. The sound behind the pieces was culled from John Zorn, David Krakauer, Anthony Coleman, Frank London, The Klezmatics, Andy Statman, Brave Old World, etc. The experience of creating TALES OF A JEWISH AMERICAN PRINCE has taught me that different music can be put behind these pieces or a creative klezmer band could compose music to go with the pieces as well.

TALES OF A JEWISH AMERICAN PRINCE

TALES OF A JEWISH AMERICAN PRINCE was first presented by Star Mountainville Group at MAKOR of the 92nd Street Y on May 18, 2004 at West 67th Street in NYC. It was directed by the author (with valuable input from Moshe Paul Mones and Jack Zeman) with the following cast:

Judah . . . . Glenn Laszlo Weiss
A Sprite, Mother, Sally, Rae, etc . . . . Norma Jean Howland

Sound was by Jonathan Delson
Dramaturgical Assistance was provided by Jack Zeman.

Music was given to the production by Frank London, David Krakauer and Andy Statman.

PART ONE

Unless indicated all dialogue is Judah.

Once upon a time there was a . . . a . . . a . . . survivor, no, no, . . . a prince . . . no, a Jewish American Prince, he heard a call . . . once upon a time . . . Hungarians, survivors, lots of them and dad, no, no, no. Once upon a . . . gave me this so called kingdom, named me Isadore after my father's father - Isser in Hebrew . . . but once upon a time . . . royalty? I prefer Judah . . . once upon a time got called Isser the pisser by kids . . . call me Judah. . . who speaks through the Jewish Blues, once upon a time dad was in the camps . . . no, no – his dad gave up his food so my dad could eat . . . see? No, no . . . once upon a time . . . he starved. Once upon a time - how about, how about . . . call me Judah, Judah Ben Judah, son of a Jew. Hey, this isn't my kingdom, is it? What is this kingdom . . . some old guy with a beard? Crying for his women? No, no, no . . . once upon a time . . . same old story . . . he disappoints . . . mother . . . wife . . . daughter . . . oh yeah, oh yeah . . . it's the Jewish blues . . .

BLUEJEW

What? Do you hear? What do they want?
The worst. I say, the worst cry you can ever hear.
Is a mother's cry. It leaves such a bitter taste.
In her son when he disappoints her.
He never gets over it. He never stops hearing the sound.

What? What do you want?
Is honesty not enough?
Is the truth too costly?
Is my suffering never in your league?
Okay, now we're getting somewhere.

Now, you hear my sound down low.
Without laughter.
My own sound of blue.
Blue. Jew.

I always had this raging conflict going on between the good Jewish boy inside me and a more questioning and rebellious one. The good one, in my mind would parade around in a flock of Black Hats, Orthodox Jews, a proud member of the first born of the Holocaust survivors. My mission clear and engrossed in absolute devotion.

OUR SOUND

Listen, listen to our sound. Hear it echo through the ages. Hear it call our people our people together. Hear it sing through the centuries of trials. Trials not by our peers.

Listen. Hear the sounds of laughter on a crowded street. Feel the hustle, the bustle to make a buck. Crowded together, people all talking at the same time. Crowded in great numbers though we are few. Listen to our sound. Voices that clamor, that clash together. Trying to put across each other's view. Rejoicing in being so few.

Choosing to walk the streets at dusk. Together, always together. Witnessing the sun going down in the distance. Seeing the light of our God and following it to its furthest point. Together, always together. Clamoring, pushing, savoring our closeness to each other. Listen to our sound. Others plot against us and scheme some nonsense but we weather the storms. They cry out to the world and rely on age-old perceptions yet we persevere. Together, though we are few. Crowded in great numbers in a little space. Like our fathers, like our grandfathers, we go on safe together and we sway to our sound. We go down the embankment as the sunset develops. We argue some Talmud and mix in a little business. Follow your gods, leave us in peace. Peace, peace. We want peace, not suspicions. Peace, peace. We want peace, not innuendoes. Into the night we wander. Crowded together in diminishing numbers, voices growing softer into the vapors of the night. Listen to us owning our sound. Together, always together, though we are few.

And then I was also the boy who stood apart. I was bored in synagogue. Feeling the religion deadening all the spirit around me. With a God defined in such stark terms of good and evil, crime and punishment, sin and piety, I couldn't help but feel there was a wheeler-dealer standing outside the gates of Heaven checking Jewish membership cards.

JEWS IN HEAVEN

Come all you Jews to Heaven.

Which Jews? All Jews. You sure? There are so many kinds of Jews, nu? Don't miss it! It's the closest thing to a country club. Golf all day. Kibbitzing in the day room. Ethical discussions in the library. Food, all the food you can savor. I told you it's like a country club. But so confusing to choose the type of Jews we want here. You got Orthodox, Conservatives, Reformed, Revisionists, Reconstructionists, Refuseniks and even some who know Jesus, emmis! I can't make a decision, I'm only security, see. Come, all of you Jews and get on board. For sure, it's relaxed here. It's like, you know, a country club atmosphere. And you know what? It's a little like The Concord. Or Colorado, but only a few of you know Colorado. And can you believe? We've got shuffleboard, too. What do you think? What kind of a place you think we're running here? And now, most important, what kind of a Jew are you? A black hat? Do you put on the tsistsis and the tfillin or what? What? Am I getting too personal or something? We must know. Are you just plain old neighborhood variety with the questions in the voice and the ability to bug all the goyim? No big deal. Doesn't really matter. We're completely relaxed here. Supper is always served on time. We're informal but as you can tell, well-informed. Thanks a lot. See you soon.

One day in early middle age, I was hit with all this buried passion, voices and opinions I didn't know I had inside of me. I heard the Jewish blues and this turmoil began its course. It was uncovered not like a buried treasure but more along the lines of distorted feelings and actions. There I stood unable to explain why such a thirst to erase the ghosts and shadows of the past lived in me and yet the creative urge to HOWL also emerged. There were the stories of my mother's father, the rabbi. Stoic, resourceful and heroic, he saved his family from the Nazis. Remarkably, he learned English well enough at fifty years of age to become a rabbi in America because it was a better gig than teaching, his previous occupation in Hungary. I can still hear my grandmother's voice singing his praises.

GRANDPA'S STORY

Listen children, I want to tell you a story.
Listen, children, children everywhere.
There was a man who had a mission.
To save his children, just like you they were.
He went into the woods a Jew.
And came out onto the street, a German baker,
The best around.
His heart was aching.
His soul seemed damned.
His pulse was quaking.
His demeanor stayed calm.
He lied to his enemy.
He had to have the remedy,
To protect the lives he brought into the world.

He used to be a teacher.
He now was a forger of passports.
He was his town's most learned man.
He now became a laborer, who worked with his hands.
He never gave up on his freedom.

He never deserted his family.
Hear O Israel, how many like him there were.
Today so precious few have arisen from the seeds.
To pray in Hebrew while cursing in German.
Finding solace in praying while playing a devil.

He went into the woods a scared Jew
And out he came a great German baker.
Wiping flour and blowing powder
Right off his white duds
As somewhere else in the air...
Flew Jewish suds.

That was one hell of a road to follow or rather quite a legacy to live up to. Then there was my father. He survived three concentration camps. He was an adolescent when the Holocaust started. He was guided by something bigger than circumstance or maybe by some great inner resource that defied the evil reality around him.

FUNNY KID

A funny kid on the run.
Getting away without murder.
His own, narrowly escaping his own.
Living on his wits and entertaining the idiots
Who follow the deadly orders.

He's missing when work starts.
Missing work is the key.
Little does he know it's his destiny.
Where is the funny yid, the funny kid?
Who runs away all the time.

Hiding in the trenches.
Diving into the ditches.

Work is only a pretense
To keep the steady flow in this marriage
Of profit and racial purity.
He's lost in the shuffle.
He can't be held long enough
For anyone to decide what to do with him.
They just laugh that he's missing a finger.
Look, he can't work today.
Then send him off to another camp.
Auschwitz, Buchenwald, a little time in Treblinka.
But when he sees that line for those number tattoos
He knows it's time to run again, that funny yid.
Funny kid, they think he's a gas.
Like a frisky pet, he saves his ass.

A funny kid on the run.
Getting away without murder.
His own, narrowly escaping his own.
Living on his wits and entertaining the idiots
Who follow the deadly orders.

Funny kid on the run.
Dodging fate and beating hate
With his quick feet and quicker smile.

And then there was our relationship. It was always painful and confusing. I wanted to fight for his lost youth and dreams. He wanted to spare
me disappointment. I was born too late to fight the Nazis. He was too
beaten to match my enthusiasm and tried to scale down my hopes and
dreams. It all hurt.

SON

He has an old face. He has my look. It's in his eyes. It's in his soul. It's in
his heart. The burning bush handed down to him is the same one hand-

ed down to me. Handed down, what a diluted mess. Believe it or not, it shrouds us both. When he hides, so do I. When I disappoint him, I can't cover unless I reach into his point of view and make light. A view I have fled all my life. Futile wish. I despise him/me. In these times.

I was told that I was important but not by him.
I was told to speak up but not by him.
I was told to get myself secure by him, by him.
(Sung cantorally)
By him, by him. Quiet. On and on.
By him, by him. Quiet. On and on.
By him, by him. Quiet. On and on and on.

When he got here he spoke five languages, only parts of them, not one whole. This they done to him. He could not communicate with others. Just work with his hands. And write endless numbers on newspapers. This was his true calling. Of course, somewhere else, that is. Another world. This one didn't exist anymore for him. To himself, he was terrified. Wouldn't you be? He gave me this fear. By himself, he felt guilty. Why, oh why, was he spared? No one else that he knew. No one else that he was connected to was saved. Just him. And he could only speak fractions of words. He could only clench his fists. Shake his head. And wonder and wander and ponder. Until it all blanked out. It's my task to get past this. And not give it to mine.

So, the battle lines were drawn inside of me. Would I become this unstoppable macher like Grandpa? Or a darting, toe the line working man like my dad? This tango of two tales played out in the wilderness that was my soul.

TANGO TALE

They were two different men
Very different from each other they were
Grandpa came out of the shtetl

With a pompous air about him.
'cause he was the big macher where he came from.

Dad was wild-eyed scared.
When he got married, he looked like the personification of Fear.
 Probably didn't want to let go of the people
Who came to his wedding.
He needed to know people, his people
Could and would stick around.

Grandpa, he went right from the shtetl
Right into the synagogue.
Congregation after congregation
He came and went, came and went.
He only learned English at fifty.
And boy, could he make speeches.
He traveled across his new country
He'd outrun the Germans
And soon he'd be outrunning his age.
There was not a retiring bone in his body.
He argued everywhere he went.
He fought about all the numbers in Deuteronomy
Prophesized the doom he'd escaped from.
He told the truth his way.
The one he'd lived through.
He stuck out his chest, he knew who he was.
He got behind a used Cadillac.
It had more miles on it than it had a right to.
Like its driver, it just kept right on going.

Dad tried to piece it together.
He felt hollow echoes reverberate through his brain.
He'd found a new family to replace the one he'd lost.
He was helped by his extended family.
Because, see, he was so fractured.

He thought only parts of thoughts.
He'd cheated death so many times.
He was still a very young man.
He was taught a trade working with his hands.
Though his hands always betrayed him.
He kept thinking of his lame pal who'd been with him in all three
camps struggle in the new country without much help and was thank-
ful.
He dared seldom to dream of the father he last saw through the vapors
Of poisoned gas.
Boom! They shot his uncle in America out of nowhere.

Boom! Grandpa had another door slammed in his face.
They met in the bustling city.
Damaged, aged and destined to go on.
They did a tango of survival
Death had been cheated at the door.
Men who knew when to cut and run.
Their faith twisted to fit whatever calamity awaited them.

A boy missing a finger.
A rabbi born out of circumstance.
Taking his chances on the outer roads of America.
While the boy picked up his dead uncle off the stone floor.
One adopts the other
Not really knowing much
Not really caring
Except for one fact.
He's a Jew and He's a Jew.
This they both knew real well.
This is what they shared together.

My father never talked about his experiences in the camps. He didn't
say what he'd been through but rather dwelled on what the world could
do to me, if I wasn't careful. "It's no joke" was a favorite refrain of his.

He was overprotective, picking me up everywhere by foot, he didn't know how to drive. He didn't know how to swim. He couldn't fix anything with his hands. I grew up missing my right ring finger just like him. Except that I had mine. Sympathetic syndrome, my Mom called it. Once we heard a noise in the bushes, my Dad and I. It was probably kids goofing around. My Dad yelled and pointed to imaginary others as if he had a virtual army with him and the figures in the dark ran away. Whenever I'm scared I think of that invisible army he created. He had no numbers on his arm like most survivors. When the Steven Spielberg people interviewed him for a documentary about Holocaust survivors, they were fascinated by this fact. They pressed for details and he was insulted. He felt they didn't believe him. Some days I'm bold like my grandpa and some days I'm shy and private like my Dad. Some days I believe in miracles. Some days I see through everything and everybody and conclude it's all lies. Some days I pursue my dreams. Some days I turn on myself. I usually walk away before I believe in something. My mother wanted me to succeed. She saw my lack of belief. She taught me this prayer.

PRAYER (TUMULT)

Open my eyes, so I can see
This tumult going on inside of me.
In due time, you say
Be patient, restless one, you say.

Quell this commotion
That is rocking my world.
Force this pounding
In my brain to pause
I ask you nice.

A tumult, a tumult that comes every night.

Forces visit me.

They upset my whole vision of life.
They tear apart my comfort.
They push my serenity to the limit.
Voices rise up in my head
And discuss questions I never asked.
Upheavals resume nightly,
Stop this madness
Before I go insane.
I never was that stable to begin with.

Haunting images call me.
Carry me to the edge.
I witness a wrinkled old man who protected them.
So two troubled people could bear me.
I was blind before but now I see.
Blind before but now I see.
Yes, blind but now I see.

(Softly)
I call myself Judah.

END OF PART ONE

PART TWO

So much of this background of pain was ignored in my youth. Oh, there was teenage pain. There was rebellion, plenty of it. There was the point of view that having European parents was not cool. They didn't understand us even more than those kids with Jewish American parents. My Dad staked us out when we partied and went through my chest of drawers when I succumbed to drugs. His interventions seemed ridiculously futile and pathetic. Today, I know he was just being a loving father. I became "Pete West" and ran off to do summer stock while a lot of my Jewish peers prepared for their law and medical careers. My aversion to my background kept growing. I became a master of the escape with a head full of learned responsibility. The carefree artistic world aided my flight from this fractured Jewish tradition I was born into. But, late at night, the roots reached out to me. I became Judah again.

THE HUNGER

Three a.m. and it's my nightly bad dream wake-up. Familiar terrain covered in repeated nightmares. Jewish sounds reverberate the walls. Jewish faces infiltrate my cool, plastic assimilated world. I peer in from outside a fence. I see a secret coded world but deep within me, I possess a key. A world of ethereal ghosts. A world where monsters dwell. A world where despots rule. A world watched over by the long hand of Justice. A world where history does cast a doubt. A world where absolute faith in nothing is advised. A world where every now and then this long hand of Justice does falter. A world of dead scrolls, a world of parted seas. Some that roar, some that angrily flow. Some that allow the faithful to flee. Some that swallow up all of the world's misery.

Jewish faces. Jewish laws. Jewish headaches. Jewish questions. Jewish dreams. Oy, this key weighs so heavy on me. What is a Jew? So many factions. So many sects. So many theories. So many texts. Different ones that huddle together. Some that are assimilated with the masses. Some so radical and militant. Some so benign and accommodating. All kinds in times of trouble. Always times of trouble, a world full of trouble, always a monster and always the search for angels. Always ghosts of ancient sages who are always watching. Jewish lives bear a lot of watching.

.

My soul knows the stories, my being knows the sounds.
My feet know the steps, my heart knows what to feel.
My rhythm comes from way back, my speech has the twists and turns.
My voice has the hully-gullies of Galilee.
My hunger for togetherness is bottomless and centuries old.

My soul knows the stories, my being knows the sounds.
My feet know the steps, my heart knows what to feel.
My rhythm comes from way back, my speech has the twists and turns.
My voice has the hully-gullies from Galilee.
My hunger for togetherness is bottomless and centuries old.

(THE HUNGER ends)

After ten years of constant drug-induced stupors…After ten years of failed attempts to make it in the theater…After ten years of relationship warfare…I awoke married, desperately confused and lacking any inner peace. I was married to Sally and she was intent on us going back to the synagogue.

(Scene between JUDAH and SALLY)

SALLY
Judah! Are you ready yet for shul?

JUDAH
I'll never be ready for shul? Sally, what's with this newly found religion?

SALLY

What's wrong with it?

JUDAH

Nothing for some people but I can't stand it. Maybe I was force-fed too much as a kid.

SALLY

Well, I've been really thinking about it lately. The community. The culture, the history. I didn't grow up with it.

JUDAH

Well I'm still getting over it.

SALLY

Very funny. No, seriously, I mean being connected to something bigger. We felt like we were on our own.

JUDAH

Sounds good to me.

SALLY

Judah, I don't want that.

JUDAH

Well, maybe I do.

SALLY

Judah, we're talking about starting a family.

JUDAH

Yeah, so.

SALLY

Yeah, so. Yeah, so. Always the same, flat, "yeah, so what?" You know something, Judah?

JUDAH

What?

SALLY

I think you're too flat.

JUDAH

Great. And who are you, Dr. Joyce Brothers?

SALLY

No, I'm pregnant.
(pause)
See, Judah, that's what I mean. Nothing, no reaction.

(Scene ends)

JUDAH

I'm stunned and can only hear my mother's voice.

MOTHER

When we were starting out, things had to fall into place. There wasn't any help for us. We were already grown up without any childhood. The things we had seen made us appreciate whatever we had. We knew a family was what we wanted. We knew we had come through it alright. We knew that we wanted the same things. We didn't analyze each other. We knew we were given Life for a reason. We knew something had to come from that. The places we ran from haunt us like wolves in the dark. We did the right thing, I'm sure, because it came from God. You hand down the best values and hope they stick.

JUDAH

As I get more and more paralyzed.

(Scene between JUDAH and SALLY resumes).

SALLY

Judah, you haven't spoken coherently to me in a week.

JUDAH

Sally, I, uh, you know…

SALLY

Well, what the hell's going on?

JUDAH

Fear. Weirdness. Paralysis.

SALLY

Oh, come on, being a father is not so bad.

JUDAH

Who said it's bad?

SALLY

Most men would be happy, optimistic.

JUDAH

I suppose I'm still flat in your book.

SALLY

I didn't say that. I didn't say that at all.

JUDAH

For once, eh, Sal?

SALLY

Never again. I've said it too many times.

JUDAH

Can I tell you something about yourself?

SALLY

What?

JUDAH

It's really, only, that is, it's just one word.

SALLY

Judah?

JUDAH

Hormones.

SALLY

Yeah, so. I'm pregnant.

JUDAH

And crazy.

SALLY

Alright.

JUDAH

And mean.

SALLY

Stop it, now. I mean it.

JUDAH

What? I thought I'm too flat to effect you.

SALLY

Very funny.

JUDAH

No, it's not.

SALLY

No, it's not. I'm tired.

(Scene Ends)

JUDAH

And meanwhile, a third generation is arriving. Floating beneath the surface like flotsam and jetsam.

(JUDAH and SALLY perform FLOTSOM AND JETSOM)

It's on the surface, on everyone's lips.
A new life is coming, a prophecy will live.

The most important mission in a Jewish person's life
Is to create, I tell you, a brand new Jewish person's life.

So few candles were left lit and the ones who survived.
Prayed for one last laugh to arise.
Against those who tried to kill them all.
Baby, we're talking about babies.
Lively, hungry, brainy Jewish babies
Guaranteed to drive a Nazi up the wall.
Jewish babies on the crawl, on the crawl.

It's all on the surface, it's on every yenta's lips.
A new life is coming, a prophecy will live.
Get ready! Sound the charge!

Lively, hungry, brainy, loud, demanding, intense Jewish baby
Is on the way.

The culture breathes
All is right with the world.
The older generation swoons.
At the latest news.
Tell the sun and hail the moon
Brainy, lively, hungry Jewish baby.
Coming soon! Coming soon!
Real soon.

(Scene between JUDAH and SALLY resumes)

JUDAH

Look, my mother said…

SALLY

I don't care what she said, I want it like this…

JUDAH

What do you mean you don't care?

SALLY

Just what I said.

JUDAH

Don't talk about her like that.

SALLY

Why don't you ever stick up for me like that?

JUDAH

Because you're wrong.

SALLY

I'm the mother of your child, you son of a bitch. I can't be wrong.

JUDAH

Oh, yeah. You sound wrong to me.

SALLY

Oh, yeah.

JUDAH

Does everything have to be your way?

SALLY

Like you even have a way? What's your big idea, huh?

JUDAH

I have ideas.

SALLY

Not about anything around here. You're always out.

JUDAH

All you ever want to do is stay in.

SALLY

So? I'm a mother now. So, go shoot me. Or is that too exciting for your flat nature?

JUDAH

Again about my nature?

SALLY

Just stay home more.

                    JUDAH

What home?

                    SALLY

Exactly. What relationship?

                    JUDAH

What love?

                    SALLY

Get out!

                    JUDAH

I'm gone.

        (Scene Ends)

Now, my wandering begins. I'm separated from my daughter. This is without an end in sight as Mother and Daughter disappear. Loss is not only in my family's past anymore. I'm haunted by my own desertion. A tumult, a Jewish love song.

        (JUDAH performs BALM FOR THE SOUL)

Oh, little wonder, my little wonder.
Your eyes are locked onto the future.
They see clearer than mine.
Far clearer than I ever saw.
The hope of seeing you is my balm for the soul.

I'm crazy about you.
But I have to let you go.
I'm crazy about you
To do what I have to do.
Crazy enough to walk the streets

With the thought of you somewhere else.
You are somewhere else tonight.

Oh, little wonder, little wonder.
My mother would have loved you.
My grandma would have praised you.
My grandpa, the rabbi would have exalted you
To his congregation.
My father would have read you stories until you slept
As hard as that would be to get you to
Go to sleep while a story is being read.
The hope of seeing you is my balm for the soul.

I'm crazy about you
But I have to let you go.
I'm crazy about you
To do what I have to do.
Crazy enough to walk the streets
With the thought of you somewhere else.
You are somewhere else tonight.

Oh little wonder, my little wonder.
Your tears are bitter like the Earth.
Your innocence parts the seas.
The force of your ideas has the reach
Of many sages that came before you.

The hope of seeing you cleanses my mind, washes my spirit, too.

I'm lost. I go into this dark cave, which is my life. I'm flailing away.

END OF PART TWO

PART THREE

Dear God, I am looking down a long hallway and I don't like what I see. Do you? It's my own chamber of horrors. It's no joke. It's real. Yet, I have to go on. I have to fight for my rights, even when I was so wrong. My heart feels so open yet I'm certainly hated. I'm vilified. By myself, most of all. Nothing and everything has prepared me for being so hated. For a Jew it's like a second nature type of thing. A reality I was brought up with, to be hated so deeply. As a father, I don't know... paralysis still. We Jews can bring such humor to this world. God, can I crack jokes when I'm hurting the most. I know what that's like. Isser the Pisser. God's a Joker. Which one are we today? How about Judah, the blues man?

BLUE JEW #2

What? Are you still here? What do you want?

The most. I say, the most heartbreaking cry you can ever hear.

Is a wife's cry. Especially when she's also a mother.

And you're bound to disappoint her.

You'll never get over it. You'll never stop hearing the sound of her sighs.

Here again? What more can I give?

Do my efforts continue to fall short?

Is the price your eternal regret?

Is my suffering never in your league?

Okay, now we're getting somewhere.

Now you hear my sound down low.

Without tears.

My own sound of blue.

Blue. Jew.

I had to put everything on hold. I had to halt the search for my daughter. Completely at a loss, I went to a Second Generation Retreat to try to resolve all this stuff inside me. Soon I got a job there as the Host of the Retreat. I drew upon Grandpa and that rabbinical background but it was out of whack. Like the blind leading the blind, I concocted some weird hybrid of the Twelve Step Programs, Woodstock and a New Age Zionism. I'll take you there up in the wilds of upstate New York. Under the tent of the Children of the Holocaust Survivors Retreat.

JUDAH AS THE HOST:
Welcome friends and neighbors to our Retreat here in Utopia. I am Judah, your Host. We embrace all of you from every walk of life, every town, every county, every race, every creed and every religion. Those of you who want to pray with us, you fulfill our basic requirement. You wish to pray with us, that's it. Here we love to mix the modern with the mystical, the strange with the stable, the old time with the sublime and the ancient with the new breed. If you will all just move over, the ushers are bringing more chairs. We are crossing the boundaries and we have visitors from all over. Here we like to speak of one world. We like to speak of people dealing with their own private choices of mitzvoth. Good deeds. We keep our own consciences and we keep our own principles intact. Yes, we abide by a code, which embraces different disciplines, beliefs and thinking, the best only from East to West. What makes us retain our Jewishness is the singing and dancing of the He-

brew tunes from our youth. This is what we love to bring to our community. Will the Band, yes, the famous rock group, come on up and to do the Rock of Ages? Thank you. And will the famous chazen, Cantor Hertzberg join them with something old and swinging from our forefathers? Yes, and can we all sway? Good. Just keep swaying and remember friends, to keep the focus on yourselves and to live by the principles and steps in your life. The only inventory you may take is your own and please no crosstalk nor negative feedback in this our healing place. (A brick is thrown followed by jeers of "dirty Jews blocking the road"). Friends, neighbors, give me a moment . . . I need to overcome those vile vibes, hold it, hold on, please, cut the music . . . You know friends it's so easy to forget here up in the beautiful clouds. Where we all can play at being Jewish cowboys and girls. It is so easy to convince ourselves that these things don't exist anymore but the sad fact is, friends, they still do. Wait a moment, friends, I am now speaking for the Jews here, I mean, can I only speak to the Jews here? Will the ushers clear the space for Jews only, I'm sorry. I know it's a drag to be polarized like this...what? Not kosher? What do you mean? Oh, the exclusion. Yes, I see what you mean but as those remarks were directed specifically at us Jews, I don't quite see . . . Solidarity? You want to express solid-well that's wonderful. What is the response? Do we accept this as a group? Mixed response. Well, this is what I meant. I don't think we have evolved to such a place yet, at this time of such forgiveness and acceptance. A shame, yes but, well that's why we need this healing space, isn't it? Now, to get back to our program, will the Moscow Art Theatre come up and give a sample of the The Dybbuk as we conclude with a very slow rendition and moving, yes, always moving, rendition of AVENU MALKENU. Live and let live, folks, even though it's a bitch. May the Promises one day enter all Anti-Semites, yeah? Now we'll conclude with a special procession of the children of survivors. But before we get into it, here's a little rap we can all relate to. I pose the question first: What does it feel like to be a Second Generation Jew?

(does SECOND GENERATION)

Boppity, boppity bop…
All I'm accustomed to. It's all that I know. Birthright of the second
generation.

Every boat springs a leak.
Every wheel rolls off.
Every attempt is a bust.
Every belief is a transparent crock.
Hopes are dashed. Bulbs are dimmed. Tests are failed. Sentiment is
dangerous. Feelings are twisted. Life moves closer to death. And around
corners are atrocities. Such terrible, terrible things.

Boppity, boppity, bop…
It's all I'm accustomed to. It's all I know. Birthright of the next generation.

Enthusiasm is easily spent.
Love exists only in the distance.
Identity drowns in confusion.
Martyrdom is for fools.
Money is logic and more of it is more logical.
Enemies abound. Suspicions are paramount. Easily understood. Just
cause. Deadly to the soul. Crushed spirit.

Boppity, boppity, bop…
It's all I'm accustomed to. It's all I know. Birthright of the children of
the damned who were saved.

My heart goes out to him.
I fight unseen enemies.
Battles that were never realized.
Nonsense that rules in a deadly reign.
Rain closely follows glorious sunlight.
Night always pokes through the days.
Severed roots gnarled so close to the surface.

Boppity, boppity, bop…
All I'm accustomed to. It's all I know; my birthright.

SECOND GENERATION ends

Okay, it does the soul good to let out the beasts within. Before we go on, I'd like to give you another spiel. A while back, I saw this Anti-Semitic cartoon of this rich fat Jew and one day I was feeling rather isolated and the cartoon started talking back to me. No shit, it came to life like some perverse float in a Nazi parade.

(Does ROLY POLY)

ROLY-POLY

Round and round the wheel of money goes into my pockets lined with fur. Priceless commodities find their way into my portfolio and don't forget the obligatory diamonds and gold. Bobbing and weaving through my pre-paid streets go all of my brothers and sisters and the world goes round and round because my money is roly-poly.

Controlling all the schemes and buffeting all the natural disasters away from me and mine and sent right over to you and yours. Doesn't it make perfect sense to all that I come up smiling in my runaway yacht as I watch the sea shimmer as I get my party to relax on the cruise I paid for, of course. Roly-poly, roly-poly.

Here I come down the street with everyone I meet bought and sold by me, of course. My servants are pawns in my game. Doesn't matter which country my ancestors fled from without a pot to piss in. Or having should I say the poverty of no freedom. Roots blown in the wind but the scourge of all societies is ME and I always get removed. Yet, here I stand, pushing all the buttons and continuing to control all of YOUR options. Irony, irony, it's roly-poly time again. Time for the pogrom. Time for the purge. Time for the chase to begin. Again. Time to prick my balloon tummy again. Time to incite the crowd and move against me once more. For all of civilization starts and ends with my machinations.

And roly-poly I roll down your cliff again. An unwanted guest with money left behind and to the victors go the spoils. I'm always so grateful to escape with my life and round ass intact, right?

(ROLY POLY ends)

And now for the more visually oriented. Here is a little video I cooked up with some friends. Judah and the New Yiddish Posse present JEWS ARE COOL.

(Judah and Rae perform JEWS ARE COOL)

JEWS ARE COOL

We've learned to brave the cold.
We've learned the hard way on Time's endless road.
We've learned through our hard-headed ways.
We've learned survival through a universal plague.

We've got the moves.
We've got the clout (Farrakhan's right).
We got the licks.
We got the tricks.

Last time we got hung out on a limb.
We were cast aside like flies.
We don't think it'll happen again.
'cause we won't let the tide turn.
Voices, voices, everywhere.
Saying, saying things

That cause fires to burn.
Under a canopy of stars we learn
Under a blanket of justice we turn
Taking care, taking care, taking care.

We maneuver, we strike, we are fully able to handle
the arrows of hatred that come our way.

We got the groove.
We got the moves.
We got our cracks…sealed.
We got our tracks…wheeled.

Believe, believe, believe it…we do.
Beehives of scapegoating will never work again.

(JEWS ARE COOL ends)

Well, that ends this part of the Retreat and now I guess I need some healing, too. Make way!

(Judah leaves Host's role and comes back to audience)

I was out of control. The demons perched in my mind, my heart and soul were all battling each other through some crazy performance catharsis. All these different sides of me. Ones that I didn't know I had inside. I was going nowhere fast. I was about to go off the deep end when I met a woman named Rae at the retreat and she helped me more than she could ever know.

SCENE BETWEEN JUDAH AND RAE

RAE

Where did all that come from?

JUDAH

I don't know. There's a lot of anger there.

RAE

Maybe you need to tell your dad's story.

JUDAH

He never spoke about it.

RAE

There must be some way to do it. You can't go around filled with bile from the past.

JUDAH

True, but it's all a puzzle. Just little glimpses, attitudes.

RAE

Still, if you do one more piece out there, I'm pretty sure every Second Generation Jew will turn into a commando to stop you.

JUDAH

On who's side?

RAE

I don't want to find out. I have an idea. Can you be your father?

JUDAH

What do you mean?

RAE

Can you give him the words he never said?

JUDAH

I thought I've been doing that.

RAE

Only in anger. I mean the story. Give the facts as best you can, piece them together.

JUDAH

No, I just want the emotions.

RAE

It's not helping.

JUDAH

No.

RAE

You've got to find a way to stop the pain from exploding.

JUDAH

I want to fight it. I can't let it happen.

RAE

But it happened. Go through it. It's the only way out.

JUDAH

I got it. There is a document.

RAE

What kind of document?

JUDAH

One composed for the reparation money.

RAE

There you go. It's the perfect thing. What's it like?

                          JUDAH

I've never been able to read it.

                          RAE

Really, why?

                          JUDAH

Couldn't face it.

                          RAE

Can't be as bad as the reality.

                          JUDAH

Well, I guess I did read it.

                          RAE

And?

                          JUDAH

It totally frustrates me.

                          RAE

Why?

                          JUDAH

There's no struggle. Just victimization.

                          RAE

So?

                          JUDAH

I can't relate to it.

                          RAE

Try to just be there for him, instead.

JUDAH

It's so remote like it happened to someone else.

RAE

Maybe it did. I mean, maybe they were all different people in the camps. Look, Eli and Sam are testifying tonight.

JUDAH

Testifying?

RAE

They're telling their folks' stories. Come and see what they get out of it and maybe you'll be able to deal with your father's story better if you testify, too.

JUDAH

And you think I'll just get up and testify, too?

RAE

How else can you stop doing this angry exploding? Got a better idea?

JUDAH

I don't know.

RAE

It'll be hard but you'll get through it.

JUDAH

And then we joined the procession of the children of the survivors and it was so powerful to feel at home among so many.
 (PAUSE)
And then Rae and I continued our work together.
The testimony of Judah. For Zolie, a blues so far removed.
 (Reads actual testimony)

*In March of 1944, Gestapo came into Csenger, Hungary on the second day
of Passover and gave out leaflets to every Jewish family that they should pack
two suitcases and all Jews to assemble in the synagogue. We stayed overnight.
In the morning they loaded us into wagons pulled by oxes and took us to
Mateszalka in the ghetto. No Jews stayed behind in Csenger. We stayed until
the middle of May. We were put into cattle wagons, about 17,000 Jews.
After 30 hours we arrived in Auschwitz. My mother took three of my siblings and I clinged to my father's hand. Later, I learned that my mother and
siblings were burned in the crematorium.*

RAE

What do you get?

JUDAH

I get nothing. They went here, there. They died, they survived. Like
mindless sheep. Drives me nuts.

RAE

Don't you feel anything?

JUDAH

I'm blocked. There's no connection. Anger's far away. I remember something, though. A vague memory.

RAE

What? From when?

JUDAH

I was a little boy. We were at a pool in Astoria, Queens. Dad and I.
Some kids pushed ahead of us on this humongous line. Dad said, "fucking Chinese". Real soft. Just like that.

RAE

So?

JUDAH

Don't you see? He was angrier than the situation warranted. Out of nothing. So mad. "Fucking Chinese". Like later, "Fucking Arabs" or … others. Somebody always stealing the bread out of his mouth.

RAE

Why would this get stuck in your mind? It's minor stuff, New York living. Happens every day.

JUDAH

It just stays with me and you know, I get angry out of nowhere just like that. Everyone just stares at me. Out of nowhere. I get it now.

RAE

How does it relate to his story of the camps?

JUDAH

He went back there at the Astoria Pool. It's the crowds, he goes back. He loses himself in the crowds. He feels like an object cast aside. I feel it, too, though it's not my experience. It's like a transfer.

RAE

I guess I can see that.

JUDAH

Like it happened to me.

RAE

Keep reading the document.

JUDAH

OK, but that anger…I don't want it around my daughter.

RAE

OK, keep going.

JUDAH

(Reading document)

My father and I, we were passed by Mengele. Then we marched into Birke-nau-Auschwitz. They shaved our heads and sent us into the shower room and after that gave us fluchtling clothing and hats. My number was 32386. After that we marched all night smelling the burning in the crematorium. We arrived in the Ziganner Lager. We stayed there two weeks. We went into the Polish Lager in Auschwitz. After two days they put us in railroad cars and we arrived in Buchenwald. We stayed in Gzelt Lager. They examined us physically, they took our history and gave us new fluchtling outfits. After two weeks they took us to Byzeitz in labor camp. Camp had bout 12 barracks next to coal and benzene manufacturing plants. Stayed there two months. Because of heavy bombing daily, we moved into another lager named either Rhinebeck or Rhinesdorf, I don't remember exactly. It was a camp about 18 barracks near a railroad station and they took us little commandos every day to search for unexploded bombs. We had 11 capos. The head capo's name was Heintz and he beat the hell out of us, every day. Later, I found out that in 1951 he was convicted in Frankfurt, Germany. We were bombarded all the time so we were dispersed and ran into a forest in Germany.

Where's the story?

RAE

It's there.

JUDAH

It is? I don't hear it. He recoils from it.

RAE

Not quite.

JUDAH

I feel him recoiling.

RAE

I don't hear that. Just walk through it with him. Be there with him. What do you see?

JUDAH

I see a long walk through dark forests. The stench of death everywhere. I feel the loss, the pain. People gone. Gone from their homes, from their towns, from whole countries. The wind howling as I walk. Inconsolable loss everywhere. I'm lost in the dark. I have no hope, I have no feeling. How do I begin life again? I swallow hard. I swallow memories. I swallow my childhood. Mother, sisters, brothers, all gone. Disappear. Swallow deep, shallow breaths. I let go of my Dad's hand and he's also gone for good. I wave goodbye like a robot. In a dream, I've gone mad and now stand still, nowhere. Rage begins slightly, put it away. Quiet. On and on. Feeling like I'm about to burst. Clamp down, it's no joke, no, never was. I search and search through the trees of the forest. Feels like forever. Me, him, God, friends, the enemy, the dirty bastards, all frozen in time. Numb, I'm dumb with loss. Can't even kill them with guns Americans give me when they find us. Where does all this rage go? Put back into life, twenty years old now. Start again. Organizations feed me, put me back together, though, with plenty of pieces missing. I go on a long trip. Relatives I never met welcome me in a strange new language. Teach me a trade. Meet a girl, fall into life. Go to synagogue again, find a new way to pray, one that has different meaning, the prayers. They're like half of what they were. They're like a half breath. Like a whisper. Full of doubts. But I go through the motions like I'm keeping my father's memory alive. I have children. I try to be a father. I'm half in, half out. Not quite in light, not in darkness. Always kind of alone. Always part of me hearing a faint echo of screams, names called, screams again following me. Just under the surface.

RAE

Yes, yes.

JUDAH

(Finishing the document)

In April we regrouped with SS guards. They marched us to Sudatenland. They put us in a lager with all people from other lagers. After four days we marched into Therezian-Stats. In Therezian-Stats, there were mainly little houses. They put us like wild men in the basement of those houses. After three weeks on May 8, 1945, we were liberated by the Russian Army. Me and others got the flag typhus and they brought us into Kassernes until I was cured. They gave us two weeks rehabilitation and I left about end of June 1945, on a train to go back to Hungary to look for my family. I realized in Hungary that I had nobody alive. With the help of Jewish organizations in August 1945, I went to Vienna. A few months later to Salzburg and then to Fernwald displaced persons camp in Germany. In 1949, I came to the United States.

RAE

How do you feel now?

JUDAH

A little lighter. But there's still a weight I'd like to lose.

RAE

Let's move on to the others who died.

JUDAH

How do we start?

RAE

Let's start with all the aunts and uncles and grandparents who never made it out of the camps.

JUDAH

Bernie, he was sixteen and a math wiz.

RAE

Like your dad.

JUDAH

Even better, supposedly. Auschwitz, gas. Dottie, she was the graceful one. She was said to have skated on singed ash. Auschwitz, the showers and with her Betty, the bashful one, who sewed such beautiful dresses for the spring festivals.

RAE

Want to take a break?

JUDAH

No, but I can only deal with two more for now. Isaac, the mournful one. He was a barber and it was said he could listen to ten men's stories a day and only sighed and shrugged his shoulders in response. But when he came home, he could mimic the men and embellish every story with such wit and insight he'd leave everyone in stitches. Shot. Dachau. And finally, my grandpa I never met. Isadore. A grim man, no sense of humor. A grim man for grim times. He saw straight and true. He knew what was going on and of course was powerless. Except to save one son. "Run, Zolie, run and smile all the time. Smile and bow until you outrun them all". It worked.

RAE

One life saved.

JUDAH

The only one. The Jewish blues. I hear them and never will the blues sound the same again.

(Both do ROLL CALL together)

Some were called, some were skipped
Most numbers came up, very few missed.

Could you even imagine their apprehension?
The lies, the rationalizations they told themselves, each other.

MORDECAI, SOLOMON, RUTHIE, BEA.
ISAAC, ISIDORE, MAGDA, ROSE.

some called, some skipped
most go, a few are missed.

BENJAMIN, BARUCH, JOAN, ESTELLE
ELIEZAR, NORMAN, GOLDIE, BELLE
WEISS, KATZ, COHEN, SCHWARTZ
ROSENBERG, LEVY, KAMINSKY, WIESEL
MOSKOWITZ, MOSCOVITZ, EISENBERG, ROSENSTEIN.

I can't imagine the horror
Can't imagine the rage mixed with bewilderment.
The hunger. The thirst.

JUDAH

See, the Americans gave him a gun on Liberation day. Said to go shoot
any Nazi he might see. He couldn't, wouldn't still. He just looked down
and counted the one finger alone left out of all the brothers and sisters
he had, they were all together the other week, together they were another lifetime ago.

RAE

(She embraces him.)
Your grandfather died after your father escaped. Your father protects
and protects his offspring beyond what is necessary to complete a circle
that will always be incomplete.

JUDAH

And what about the self-denial? The repeated you first, the after yous?

RAE

That's the way it lives on in us, the children.

JUDAH

And we can't quite grasp the way it all works out. But we flail away at…I mean we fight the ghosts of…I mean, we him, me, we punish others, ourselves, all in the name of something we only turn on ourselves. A futile stab at something…justice, maybe. It's not there. He does it. I do it.

RAE

It's love. Judah, you love your father.

JUDAH

He's got the self-denial, too.

RAE

Of course he does.

JUDAH

But to go on…

RAE

We must go on.

JUDAH

And they must too.

RAE

Yes, they must.

JUDAH

I love you.

RAE

Not so fast.

(JUDAH ALONE)

I cried. I ran. I prayed and cried. And when it was over I felt like I had crossed into another zone. My wandering was coming to an end. I knew my place in the world for the first time. I stopped raging and I stopped trying to live all these lives for all the dead and the ones who survived. I celebrated the love I had for the music of my people. I celebrated the spirit of their survival. I loved the people in my life and the ones in my head. One day, I decided to love them all. And the fighting ended. The battle within me died a little bit at a time. Isser and Judah became one. I learned it is all right to be confused. It's all right to have anger and not understand it. I didn't want to destroy any more. I've experienced both crying and laughing at the same moment. It has happened three times so far. When my child was born and I first held her. When I completely realized a work of art. And when I told my father I would be all right. That I could survive disappointment and he didn't have to worry anymore. It was when I told my father I'd grown up and had a chance to be happy. That was when the tumult ended and I could begin to live.

But still I was left alone mourning the family I left and hoping for another chance to make amends and see my daughter. Her name was Rivkah and it had been years now. I felt the loss and whatever acceptance I had gained didn't heal the nightly despair.

Finally I contacted my wife, Sally through her lawyer. I sent her and Rivkah an appeal for forgiveness. I detailed the demons that had plagued me. I reviewed the pressures I faced and the responsibility of bringing a child of the Third Generation into this world and how I froze. I let them know what I had learned and pleaded for mercy. Sally was finally moved. She granted me visitation for the first time. Rivkah was now ten years old. My wandering ended when I found her again.

I had written a song in the hope of finally reaching this moment. It's called Memories of Rivkah.

MEMORIES OF RIVKAH

Down by a flowing river that led to a cleansing stream I spied her waiting by the bright blue water. I was speechless. Taken aback. I was lost at the sight of her. Her crinkly smile flattened me like a potato pancake. Rivkah was her name. Rivkah. Centuries of wisdom deserted me. Evolution had left me behind. She was sitting on the banks of the river. My heart flew up and got caught in the trees. Along the riverbank, Rivkah. My grandpa would have liked her. The rebbetzen, his wife, too. My father would have adored her. Yeah, even my mother, too. The shame I brought them to not even see their granddaughter. Rivkah, what can I say? Where have you gone? I lost my soul without you. Thought I'd always be with you in your youth. Instead you disappeared while I was away.

The wind blows its empty song through the reeds. It's not as hollow as my voice, not as insane as my rotten behavior. You vanished on the first of the year just when I got confused. I was ready to conquer the world for you, Rivkah. You haunt me now. You're just a memory, now. I lost you just yesterday but it was ten years ago today. Rivkah, I still see you. Still feel you. We were to be together but you were taken when I failed your mother. I didn't stand with you but the world is not a fair place. Forgive me, Rivkah, do you forgive me? Now, I stand by the water and still see your reflection and I know you see me in your mind's eye. You can't see me yet but I have always seen you. You are somewhere I can't follow. I come from ethical people but I didn't fulfill my obligations. I was blinded by rage. Ignorance. I have roamed this world looking for another chance. I've searched for you. I promise to be more careful, more practical. Oh Rivkah, I learned how to cry these last ten years. I finally see you. Hello, Rivkah, hello. You look well. I'm so happy to see you, to really see you.

BLACKOUT

www.ingramcontent.com/pod-product-compliance
Lightning Source LLC
Chambersburg PA
CBHW021109090426
42738CB00006B/574